AVENGING ANGEL

John Brown's Raid on
Harpers Ferry 1859

RON FIELD

First published in Great Britain in 2012 by Osprey Publishing,
Midland House, West Way, Botley, Oxford, OX2 0PH, UK
44-02 23rd Street, Suite 219, Long Island City, NY 11101, USA

E-mail: info@ospreypublishing.com

Osprey Publishing is part of the Osprey Group

A CIP catalog record for this book is available from the British Library

Print ISBN: 978 1 84908 757 5
PDF ebook ISBN: 978 1 84908 758 2
ePub ebook ISBN: 978 1 78200 324 3

Index by Marie-Pierre Evans
Typeset in Sabon
Map by bounford.com
3D BEVs by Alan Gilliland
Originated by PDQ Digital Media Solutions, Bungay, UK

Printed in China through Worldprint Ltd.

12 13 14 15 16 10 9 8 7 6 5 4 3 2 1

Osprey Publishing is supporting the Woodland Trust, the UK's leading
woodland conservation charity, by funding the dedication of trees.

www.ospreypublishing.com

ACKNOWLEDGMENTS

The author would like to thank the following for their generous help: Peter
Harrington, Curator, Anne S. K. Brown Military Collection, Providence,
Rhode Island; Nancy Sherbert, Acquisitions Archives, Kansas State
Historical Society; Alan Kirby-Woolmore, Scala Archives; Patricia M. Boulos,
Digital Programs Librarian, Boston Athenaeum; Susan Grinols, Director of
Photo Services and Imaging, Fine Arts Museums of San Francisco; Michelle
Hammer, Museum Specialist, Harpers Ferry National Historical Park; David
Sullivan; and Larry Williford.

CONTENTS

INTRODUCTION

On November 7, 1837, a 39-year-old tanner from Connecticut called John Brown stood up in a prayer meeting in Hudson, Ohio, and publicly vowed, "Here, before God, in the presence of these witnesses, from this time, I consecrate my life to the destruction of slavery!" This solemn vow in response to the murder of abolitionist newspaper editor Elijah P. Lovejoy by a pro-slavery mob at Alton, Illinois, set Brown on the path to "martyrdom," and he was ultimately viewed by many in the North as the "avenging angel" determined to punish those responsible for the perpetuation of slavery in the United States. His zeal to achieve freedom for all African Americans eventually led to the monumental raid on Harpers Ferry (originally known as Harper's Ferry), Virginia, on October 16–18, 1859, which failed to spark off the expected slave revolt but did much to hasten the Civil War in America which began in 1861 and culminated in the abolition of slavery in 1865.

John Brown was born on May 9, 1800, in a humble farmhouse at Torrington, in Litchfield County, Connecticut, and was the fourth of eight children born to Owen and Ruth Brown. Although both his father and grandfather, Captain John Brown, had fought to secure the future of the US in the American Revolutionary War, the future abolitionist was raised in precarious circumstances. As with thousands of families in southern New England during the first part of the 19th century, the Browns were victims of the man-land crisis caused by the subdivisions of land, which meant that even eldest sons inherited too little to sustain a family farm. As a result, the Browns moved to Hudson, Ohio, in 1805, where Owen Brown opened a tannery. Aged 18, his son John Brown left home and went to Plainfield, Massachusetts, to enroll at the school of the Rev. Jeremiah Hallock in preparation for studying to become a Congregationalist minister. However, lack of money and problems with eyesight, termed as an "inflammation of the eyes," forced him to give up his studies and return to Hudson, where he taught himself "common Arithmetic" and the rudiments of land surveying.

1790s

The "Underground Railroad" begins to help slaves escape north

While following his father into the tanner's trade, John Brown married Dianthe Lusk, the pious 19-year-old daughter of his housekeeper, in 1820. The first six children produced via this union were raised by Brown with "a rod in one hand and the Bible in the other." For example, on one occasion after punishing his first-born son John Jr with lashes from "a nicely prepared blue-beech switch," he gave his son the whip, took off his shirt, and insisted that the boy beat him in return in order that he might learn that the "innocent" should suffer for "the collective guilt of sinful humankind." As her family grew, Dianthe showed signs of mental instability and suffered increasing ill health. She died giving birth to a seventh child in 1832. Within a year, the 33-year-old Brown married Mary Ann Day, the 16-year-old daughter of a blacksmith, and a further 13 children were produced via this second union.

The family life of John Brown was set against a period of intense religious revival called the "Second Great Awakening." (The "First Great Awakening" took place in America in the 1730s and 1740s.) In order to come to terms with westward expansion and the accompanying spread of slavery, plus the beginnings of the US Industrial Revolution, Americans began to flock to evangelical religious revivals where dramatic religious conversions took place. Meanwhile, Brown remained influenced by the Puritan beliefs of his father which focused on the pursuit of personal righteousness. His God was one of wrath and justice, not forgiveness. This ensured the vengeful nature of his pursuit to achieve the abolition of slavery in the years to come. He withdrew his membership from the Congregational church in the 1840s and never officially joined another church.

In 1835, John Brown moved to Franklin Mills, Portage County, Ohio, where for the next five years he raised cattle and sheep. Like thousands of others, he faced financial ruin as a result of the economic crisis of 1839 and tried various business ventures in an attempt to get out of debt. By the mid-1840s he had built a reputation as an expert in cattle and sheep breeding, and in 1846 entered into a successful partnership with Colonel Simon Perkins of Akron, Ohio. During the next few years Perkins and Brown began to profit from commission earned acting as agents for the wool producers of northern Ohio. Subsequently faced with opposition from the mill owners of New England who objected to dealing with middle men, Perkins and Brown attempted to create a viable market in Europe by shipping 200,000 lbs of wool to London, only to see it sell for half price following which it was shipped back to Boston. The European venture

Photographed circa 1846–47 by African American photographer Augustus Washington, this daguerreotype is the earliest known image of John Brown. He stands with one hand raised, as if repeating the pledge he had made several years earlier to dedicate his life to the destruction of slavery. With his other hand, he grasps what is thought to be the flag of the "Subterranean Pass-Way," which represented the idea of a secret escape route for slaves which reached 2,000 miles along the Appalachian Mountains and into the Deep South as far as Georgia. (National Portrait Gallery, Smithsonian Institute NPG 96.123)

ruined both Perkins and Brown, and their business partnership ended amicably in 1854.

While Brown was a failure in business, his belief in the wrongness of slavery only grew stronger. In 1847 he met the black abolitionist leader Frederick Douglass for the first time in Springfield, Massachusetts. Of that encounter Douglass stated that although Brown was white, he was "in sympathy a black man … as though his own soul had been pierced with the iron of slavery." It was on this occasion that Brown first outlined to Douglass his plan to lead a war to free the slaves. In 1849 wealthy philanthropist and social reformer Gerrit Smith had made available for settlement to free African Americans wilderness he owned in the Adirondack Mountains of New York State. Claiming that he wished to set an example to his black neighbors as "a kind of father to them," John Brown requested and was given 244 acres of this land at North Elba, near Lake Placid. In reality, he hoped to gather recruits for his future plans to overthrow slavery.

ORIGINS

During the first two decades of the 19th century, the organized opposition to slavery in the United States was limited to small groups of free blacks, Quakers, and the American Colonization Society. Founded in 1816 by Henry Clay, John Randolph, and Richard Bland Lee, the latter organization attempted to achieve the gradual voluntary emancipation of slaves and their "repatriation" to West Africa. In 1829 free black Bostonian David Walker published his *Appeal in Four Articles* which opposed the Colonization movement for deporting blacks to a continent that many of them never knew and called for a violent overthrow of slavery. A dealer in "New and second-handed Clothing," Walker sewed his *Appeal* into the lining of garments sold to black sailors for distribution along the Atlantic seaboard. White reformers such as William Lloyd Garrison were also influenced by Walker's *Appeal*. A product of evangelical reform, Garrison published the first issue of *The Liberator* on January 1, 1831, in which he declared that slavery was a national sin and demanded immediate emancipation stating, "I am in earnest. I will not equivocate – I will not excuse – I will not retreat a single inch – AND I WILL BE HEARD!" Influenced by such developments, the slave rebellion in Southampton County, Virginia, led by black lay preacher Nat Turner during August of that year, resulted in 55 white deaths and a white backlash in which about 120 African Americans were slaughtered.

Although the work of the white abolitionist movement remained on the fringe of American politics, it continued to generate a violent response in both the North and the South. Author of *American Slavery as It Is: Testimony of a Thousand Witnesses*, Theodore Dwight Weld was known as the "most mobbed man in America" because of the furious opposition he faced wherever he spoke against slavery in Ohio, Pennsylvania, and New York. In 1835, William Lloyd Garrison was forced to seek refuge in the city jail when an anti-abolitionist mob threatened to lynch him in Boston. Two years earlier, he had joined forces with Massachusetts-born businessman and

The murder of newspaper editor Elijah P. Lovejoy by a pro-slavery mob at Alton, Illinois, on November 7, 1837, set John Brown on the path of abolition that led to the raid on Harpers Ferry in 1859. (*The Martyrdom of Lovejoy*, 1881)

philanthropist Arthur Tappan to form the American Anti-Slavery Society, which spawned the Liberty Party in an unsuccessful attempt to pursue an abolitionist agenda through the political process.

John Brown's commitment to the abolition of slavery in America was probably due to the influence of his father, who was a member of the Board of Trustees of Oberlin College, an experimental school founded in 1833 by Presbyterian ministers John Jay Shipherd and Philo P. Stewart which was dedicated to anti-racism and coeducation. The Brown family was also involved with the "Underground Railroad," the abolitionist escape route for slaves begun in Philadelphia in the 1790s, and as a young man John Brown traveled around northeastern Ohio guiding fugitives to freedom. It is possible that he first read *The Liberator* at his father's house during 1833. Although he began to subscribe to that newspaper, he disagreed with its editor's beliefs that mankind could be perfected, insisting that this was a condition enjoyed only by God, and that mankind would need to be made to accept the equality of the races. This disagreement did much to shape the path Brown was to follow, which incorporated violence and force and ultimately led to the raid on Harpers Ferry in October 1859.

Bleeding Kansas

As a result of the Kansas–Nebraska Act of 1854, which organized new land for settlement in the Mid West and returned the issue of slavery to center stage in American politics, hostility grew between pro- and anti-slavery settlers in Kansas Territory. Among the latter was John Brown, Jr, the eldest son of John Brown, who felt threatened as pro-slavery forces gathered around him. Hence, Brown senior left his debts and financial woes behind

MAY 1856

"Border Ruffians" sack Lawrence, Kansas

and, financed by Gerrit Smith, headed for Brown's Station in Kansas to help his son. On the way he enlisted the aid of four of his other sons, Jason, Owen, Frederick, and Salmon, who ranged in age from 18 to 33. Thus, John Brown committed himself to a new life as a full-time fighter in the war against slavery which would end four years later on the gallows at Charlestown, Virginia.

In March 1855 thousands of pro-slavery Missourians known as "Border Ruffians" illegally crossed the state line to help elect a pro-slavery territorial legislature in Kansas Territory. Meeting at Lecompton, this body passed a draconian series of laws essentially outlawing anti-slavery in the territory. In response, anti-slavery or Free-State settlers, which included John Brown Jr, created an alternative anti-slavery legislature at Topeka, Kansas. Soon after his arrival at Brown's Station, the elder John Brown learned that a pro-slavery Virginian had murdered a Free-State settler near Hickory Point. As a result, he and his sons joined the Free-State forces gathering at Lawrence, 30 miles north of Brown's Station. As they arrived in front of the Free State Hotel at Lawrence, they were described by Scottish-born reporter for the Missouri *Democrat* James Redpath as "all standing in a small lumber wagon. To each of their persons was strapped a short, heavy broadsword. Each was supplied with a goodly number of fire-arms and navy revolvers, and poles were standing endwise around the wagon box, with fixed bayonets pointing upwards. They looked really formidable, and were received with great *eclat*."

Using some of his old skills and knowledge, John Brown traveled through Kansas Territory employing himself as a government surveyor which, according to Free-Soil settler James Hanway, gave him an opportunity to "run his compass into the pro-slavery camps," where the "ruffians took it

The caning of abolitionist Senator Charles Sumner by pro-slavery Congressman Preston Brooks on May 22, 1856, served as a catalyst for revenge for John Brown. Based on an original sketch possibly made by Winslow Homer, this depiction shows an enraged Brooks about to deliver the seated Sumner a heavy blow with his cane. At left is Brooks' fellow South Carolinian Representative Lawrence M. Keitt, raising his own cane menacingly to prevent possible intervention by the other legislators present. (Library of Congress. LC-USZC4-12985)

for granted that all surveyors were pro-slavery and opposed to the 'abolitionists' … believing that the administration would only employ those faithful to the slavery cause." Back among the Free-Soil community, he was appointed a captain and given command of a small militia group called the Liberty Guards, which consisted mainly of his sons.

Believing that the armed force of Free-Soilers gathering in Lawrence represented an "open rebellion" against the pro-slavery laws of the territory, the pro-slavers mobilized their militia and once again invited the aid of the "Border Ruffians" from Missouri. Together they massed near Lawrence, forming the "Army of Law and Order of Kansas Territory" and spoiling for a fight. Trouble was avoided on this occasion when a deal was brokered whereby the Free-State militia agreed to abide by the pro-slavery laws in return for which the "Border Ruffians" retreated back into Missouri. During the following months the Free-State population in Kansas grew as anti-slavery immigrants armed with Sharps rifles, or "Beecher's bibles," provided by Henry Ward Beecher, of the New England Emigrant Aid Society, continued to arrive in the territory. Trouble again erupted during the spring of 1856 when both pro-slavery and Free-State governments convened and began to enact competing legislature. Once more the "Border Ruffians" massed along the Missouri state line, threatening to attack the Free-State stronghold at Lawrence. When the news reached Brown's Station on May 22 of that year, Captain Brown mobilized his Liberty Guards and set out for Lawrence. Arriving too late, he found that the Missourians had already sacked the town, destroyed the presses of the *Herald of Freedom* and *Kansas Free State*, and completely leveled with cannon fire the anti-slavery headquarters at the Free State Hotel.

Anxious to avenge the sack of Lawrence, Brown also learned several days later of a vicious attack in the US Senate on anti-slavery Senator Charles Sumner by pro-slavery Congressman Preston Brooks. Angered over a speech entitled "The Crime against Kansas," and incensed by insulting remarks made about his uncle, a senator from South Carolina, Brooks had beaten the Massachusetts senator unconscious with a heavy walking cane. According to Salmon Brown, second-eldest child by his second marriage, John Brown went crazy when he received this news, adding, "It seemed to be the finishing, decisive touch." Brown himself declared, "We must fight fire with fire. Something must be done to show these barbarians that we, too, have rights."

An act of revenge came swiftly. On May 24, 1856, he assumed the role of the "avenging angel" and, accompanied by his fifth-eldest son Frederick, led an attack on a pro-slavery settlement at Pottawatomie Creek during which five settlers were dragged from their cabins and murdered with broadswords embossed with the American eagle. None of the victims were slaveholders, although several were members of the pro-slavery Law and Order Party. While John Brown never formally confessed to these killings and denied he was even present during the action, some accounts claim that he personally shot one of the victims in the head to make sure he was dead. None of those responsible for the "Pottawatomie Creek Massacre" were caught and punished, although his two eldest sons, John Brown, Jr, and

The destruction of the Free State Hotel at Lawrence, Kansas, on May 21, 1856, enraged John Brown and contributed to his revenge attack at Pottawatomie Creek three days later. This engraving showing the ruins of the Free State Hotel was based on a contemporary daguerreotype photograph produced shortly after these events. (*Kansas: Its Interior and Exterior Life*, 1856)

Jason Brown, who were not involved, were arrested by a US Marshal and placed in the custody of a company of US Dragoons. Chained together with iron fetters around their ankles, they were held in camp for several weeks before being forced to march 65 miles to Tecumseh, Kansas, to face trial. Although Jason Brown was released relatively quickly, John Brown Jr was imprisoned until September 1856, during which time he became mentally unstable, and did not recover until after his release. Highly polished by "constant exercise while raving to be released," his six-foot length of iron chain was, according to a report in the *Jamestown Journal*, of New York, eventually presented to abolitionist Henry Ward Beecher as a relic of the struggle against slavery in Kansas. Press coverage of the violent events in Kansas spread the fame of "the notorious Captain John Brown." Suppressing the facts, some abolitionist and Republican newspapers claimed that he had acted in righteous self-defense, and consolidated the myth of John Brown as an avenging angel. The Pottawatomie Creek Massacre also unleashed further fighting between Free-State and pro-slavery factions known as "Bleeding Kansas," which resulted in a total of 55 deaths, plus countless casualties. Although the conflict was brought to a temporary conclusion when US troops were called in to enforce a ceasefire toward the end of 1856, and Kansas entered the Union as a free state in 1861, warfare continued along the Kansas/Missouri border throughout the Civil War.

On the run with a price on his head following the murders at Pottawatomie Creek, John Brown and his small guerrilla band initially hid near Ottawa

John Brown's fourth-eldest son Frederick was killed by pro-slavery forces during the battle of Osawatomie, on the banks of the Marais des Cygnes River, in August 1856. (*Beyond the Mississippi,* 1867)

MAY 24, 1856

John Brown involved in the Pottawatomie Creek Massacre

Creek. Following a visit to their hideaway, James Redpath wrote "a dozen horses were tied, all ready saddled for a ride for life, or a hunt after Southern invaders. A dozen rifles and sabers were stacked around the trees … and two fine-looking youths were standing, leaning on their arms, on guard near by." Their commander "stood near the fire, with his shirt-sleeves rolled up, and a large piece of pork in his hand… He was poorly clad, and his toes protruded from his boots." Further skirmishes at Black Jack and Osawatomie consolidated the reputation of John Brown as a fearsome guerrilla fighter. At Black Jack he captured H. Clay Pate, a pro-slavery Deputy US Marshal who was attempting to hunt him down. He was less successful in August 1856, where his fourth-eldest son Frederick was killed by pro-slavery forces that destroyed Osawatomie, a small Free-State town bordered by Pottawatomie Creek and the Marais des Cygnes River. By October of that year, Brown was ill with dysentery and hunted by countless federal marshals and bounty hunters. Leaving Kansas accompanied by four of his sons, who had become disillusioned by the fighting, he headed east via Chicago, Illinois, promising to return if his health permitted and the troubles continued. But he was to formulate other plans for his war against slavery.

THE PLAN

Known as "Old Brown" or "Pottawatomie Brown" by 1857 due to his exploits in Kansas, John Brown gained an important convert to his cause when he met Franklin Sanborn, secretary of the Massachusetts State Kansas Committee. First acquainted with Brown while visiting Kansas to assess the strength of Free-State activity, Sanborn had encouraged the fugitive abolitionist to return back east. Arriving in New England, John Brown spent the next ten months raising money to equip an abolitionist military force by speaking at anti-slavery meetings and rallies. He also made an appeal to the Massachusetts Legislature in a futile attempt to secure an appropriation of $100,000 to "save Kansas as a free state."

But with the situation out west less volatile, Brown's attention shifted to his larger scheme to overthrow slavery throughout the US and he began to update his plans for the "Subterranean Pass-Way," his militant counterpart to the Underground Railroad. This involved extending the latter more than 1,000 miles farther south through Virginia, the Carolinas, and Georgia, thereby establishing a series of mountain strongholds from which to rescue fugitives or runaways, and wage war on plantation owners either side of the Appalachians. The essential difference between the "Subterranean Pass-Way" and the Underground Railroad was that the rescued slaves would be settled in or near to a northern or western American community rather than being delivered into Canada where they would exist under the British flag.

The idea for the "Subterranean Pass-Way" had originally struck Brown in 1840 while surveying lands granted to Oberlin College in western Virginia. During a meeting with black abolitionist leader Frederick Douglass at Springfield, Ohio, seven years later, he described his plan as being "to take at first about twenty-five picked men, and begin on a small scale; supply them with arms and ammunition, and post them by squads of five on a line of twenty-five miles. The most persuasive and judicious of these shall go down to the fields from time to time, as opportunity offers, and induce the slaves to join them, seeking and selecting the restless and daring.

One of the founders of the American Anti-Slavery Society and publisher of *The Liberator*, William Lloyd Garrison was opposed to the path of violence chosen by John Brown and his supporters. (Library of Congress LC-USZ62-10320)

With care and skill ... one hundred good men could be gotten together, able to live hardily, well armed, and quick to seize all advantages." His original 25 men would supply "competent partisan leaders." When his 100 were "secured, entrenched in the mountains ... the area of work would be extended, slaves run off in large numbers and from various directions, while retaining the hardy and brave fighting men." By waging such a predatory war, he hoped to harass and paralyze the people along the Blue Ridge, through Virginia and Tennessee into Alabama, so that the whole South would become alarmed and slavery made so insecure that the slaveholders themselves, for their own safety and that of their families, would be compelled to emancipate their slaves. It was also a part of his plan to seize the prominent slave-owners and hold them as prisoners either for "the purposes of retaliation," or as hostages for the safety of himself and his band, to be ransomed only upon the surrender of a specified number of their slaves, who were to be given their freedom in exchange for that of their masters. Apart from encouraging a guerrilla slave rebellion in the South, Brown predicted that free blacks in the Northern states and Canada would rally to the cause once the news spread, enabling him to establish a new, bi-racial constitutional republic.

During his wool-selling trip to Europe in 1848, Brown furthered his ideas by studying military strategy and making plans for a new style of forest fortification to be used by fugitive slaves once set free. According to journalist and fellow abolitionist Richard J. Hinton, while in Britain, Germany, Austria, and France, he "visited forts, studied ... ordnance, [and] carefully looked at soldiers and their equipments..." Based on this experience, Brown made drawings of forts to be "used in ravines or 'draws' when so situated that passage from one to another could be made. It was intended to conceal them by trees and thickets, place them on hillsides, and otherwise arrange them as ambuscades." Brown also read all he could about insurrectionary warfare. This included Plutarch's account of the stand made for years by Quintus Sertorius in Iberia against Rome, and that against the US by Osceola in the Everglades of Florida, plus that so successfully fought by Toussaint Louverture and Dessalines in St. Domingo. He likewise regarded his own bloody experiences in Kansas as a series of practical lessons on the skirmish line, and began to believe himself to be an appointed agent of God chosen to punish those who perpetuated the evils of slavery.

In order that these far-fetched plans could be funded, Franklin Sanborn introduced Brown to several other influential abolitionists in the Boston area. These consisted of wealthy merchant and businessman George L. Stearns, chairman of the Massachusetts State Kansas Committee; Thomas Wentworth Higginson, a Harvard graduate, and disunion abolitionist who believed in ending slavery, even if it led to civil war; Dr. Samuel Gridley Howe, who also helped found the Massachusetts Emigrant Aid Company to settle Kansas with Free-State settlers; the Rev. Theodore Parker, a controversial Transcendentalist minister; and Gerrit Smith, with whom Brown was already acquainted. Together with Sanborn himself, this group later became known as the "Secret Six" and funded the raid on Harpers Ferry of 1859. Money raised with their help provided Brown with 200 each of Sharps rifles and Maynard pistols, plus 4,000 cartridges and 31,000 percussion caps. These munitions were transported west and eventually stored at Tabor, in southwestern Iowa. The home of numerous other abolitionists, that place had also served as a staging point for Free-State settlers moving into Kansas. When John Brown eventually settled on his plans to attack Harpers Ferry, these weapons were shipped back east to Chambersburg, Pennsylvania, and then to the Maryland farm where he and his "army" would make final preparations for the raid. Although the Sharps weapons were used during the events of October 16–18, 1859, the pistols remained at the farmhouse as the percussion caps needed to fire them had been left at Tabor.

Regarding the provision of other arms, John Brown declared during a gathering in Boston that he held great contempt for the Sharps rifle as a weapon for inexperienced fighting men. He insisted that with "a pike, or bow and arrows, he could arm recruits more formidably than with patent guns." Visiting relatives in Collinsville, Connecticut, during the early spring of 1857, he exhibited some weapons that he claimed to have captured from H. Clay Pate at the battle of Black Jack. Among these was a dirk, or bowie knife, with an eight-inch blade that, if attached to a pole six feet in length, he considered would make "a capital weapon." During March 1857, he contracted with blacksmith Charles Blair, of Collinsville, to make 1,000 pikes at $1 each, to be completed within three months. As Brown was unable to pay the required full amount before returning to Kansas, these weapons would remain in Connecticut until 1859 by which time the outstanding amount was paid, and they were shipped to Chambersburg addressed to "J. Smith & Sons," with blades, guards and ferrules packed separately in boxes and staffs tied in bundles of 25 marked "fork handles."

Also while visiting New York City during March 1857, Brown was introduced to Colonel Hugh Forbes, a British mercenary who had aided Garibaldi during the failed Italian revolution of 1848–49. The author of a military treatise entitled *Manual for the Patriotic Volunteer; On Active Service in Regular and Irregular War; Being the Art and Science of Obtaining and Maintaining Liberty and Independence*, published in New York in 1856, Forbes was hired by Brown as a drillmaster for the force he intended to raise. Having read a copy of his *Manual* while in Kansas, Brown asked

John Brown was heavily involved in operating the escape route for slaves, called the "Underground Railroad," in Ohio during the 1830s. Painted by Charles T. Webber in 1893, *The Underground Railroad* features three leading abolitionists operating in southwestern Ohio during the 1850s. Reputedly the "President" of the Underground Railroad, Quaker Levi Coffin stands in the wagon at the rear, his wife Catherine helps the elderly African American into a farmhouse, while Hannah Haydock looks on at left. (Library of Congress LC-USZ62-28860)

Forbes to write a tactical handbook for his "troops." The mercenary thus demanded a $100 a month salary to help support his family back in Italy plus an expense account, to which Brown agreed. The two men arranged to meet in Tabor, Iowa, that summer where Brown promised his army would await training.

Before departure for Iowa, Forbes composed a one-page statement in response to Brown's request for a handbook, entitled "The Duty of a Soldier" which he addressed to "the Officers & Soldiers of the U.S. Army in Kansas." In this he stated, "Right is that which is good, true, honorable, just, humane, self-sacrificing – it is the precise opposite to wrong." Brown could not have agreed more, and saw Forbes as yet another believer in the wrongness of slavery, even though the Briton did not actually share his unyielding belief in the equality of the races.

Forbes arrived at Tabor during August 1857 to find only Brown and his third-eldest son Owen there. To make matters worse, disagreement followed over how the slave rebellion should take place with Forbes stating vaguely that "a series of slave stampedes" should be organized along "the Southern slave frontier" while, according to a later report in the *Alexandria Gazette* dated October 31, 1859, Brown insisted that a single "slave quarter in Virginia" should be attacked by a small, well-armed group with spare weapons sufficient to arm liberated blacks. The place he chose to attack was Harpers Ferry. His principal reasons for choosing that point were three-fold. Firstly, the presence of a large slave population in what was known as "the

While fighting for the Free-State cause in Kansas Territory during 1856–57, John Brown found allies in irregulars led by Jim Lane and James Montgomery. This engraving was published in the *New York Illustrated News* in 1860. (Author's collection)

Lower Valley," which consisted of that portion of the great valley of Virginia embraced within the angle formed by the Potomac and Shenandoah rivers before their confluence at Harpers Ferry. Secondly, the proximity of the Blue Ridge range of mountains with their rocky recesses and densely wooded slopes would provide comparative safety from pursuit and better enable him to protect himself from attack. Thirdly, the location at Harpers Ferry of the US Armory and Arsenal, plus the lower Hall Island Rifle Factory, held many thousand stands of arms without sufficient guard to protect them. Thus, what began as a plan to slowly deprive the South of its black labor force had become a scheme to awaken the nation to the evils of slavery via one violent and audacious raid.

When Hugh Forbes discovered that Brown was unable to pay him the monthly salary he had requested, he quit and returned to New York, promising to establish a training camp in Ohio if Brown eventually raised sufficient funds. Meanwhile, by November 1857 Brown had begun to gather at Tabor a small group of volunteers for his "army" which, besides his son Owen, included John H. Kagi, John E. Cook, Charles P. Tidd, Jeremiah Anderson, Albert Hazlett, Aaron Stevens, and William H. Leeman. During January 1858, he left these men in Tabor and traveled east through Ohio to Rochester, New York, to meet with Frederick Douglass. En route he learned that a disgruntled Forbes had attempted to contact those he believed to be supporting and financing Brown's plans, including some of the "Secret Six," in order to discredit him. As a result, Brown was forced to postpone his attack on Harpers Ferry. He grew a beard and assumed yet more aliases in order to hide his identity. He also used the delay

Possibly photographed in Kansas in 1856, John Brown had yet to grow the beard he needed to disguise his appearance after the exposure of his plans to begin a slave revolt. According to his biographer James Redpath, his dress was "extremely plain; never in the fashion, and never made of fine cloth," but he was as "tidy, both in person and dress, as any gentleman of Boston." (Boston Athenaeum)

HARPERS FERRY AND VICINITY

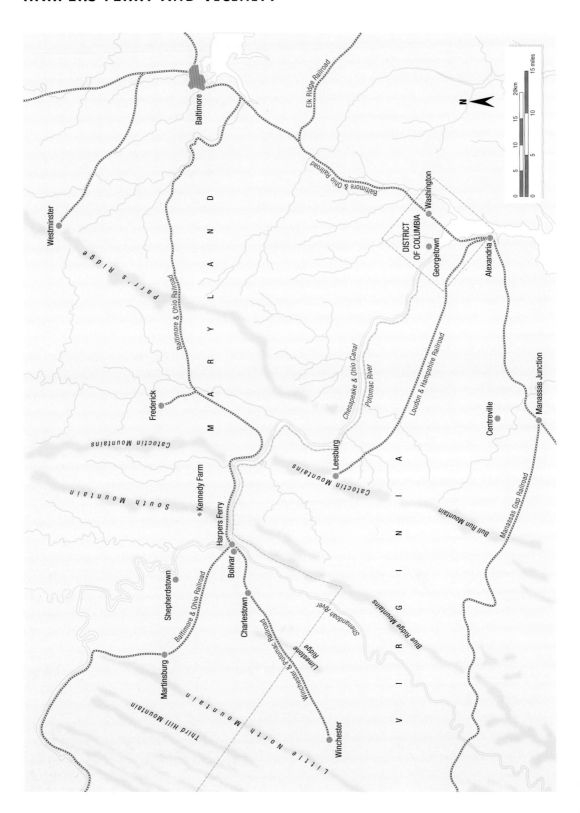

to recruit and train more men, and gathered valuable information about Harpers Ferry by allowing John Cook to live in the vicinity for about a year before the raid, during which time he gathered much information about the Armory and the local slaves.

Early in May 1858, John Brown gathered his followers together in Chatham, Canada, which was home to numerous free and fugitive African Americans who had escaped from slavery via the "Underground Railroad." There he held a secret "constitutional convention" to ratify the new constitution he had spent many months preparing, which would give legitimacy to the government he intended to create. On May 8, he addressed an audience of about 50 individuals, comprised of his white recruits plus more than 30 blacks. As a result, the meeting adopted a Provisional Constitution consisting of a 48-article document by which the group would be governed while "the war of liberation" was underway. He also ensured that most of his small group of followers were elected as "officers" of his yet

MARCH 1857

Brown orders 1,000 pikes for his guerrilla war

MAY 1858

Brown establishes his "army" in Canada with about 50 volunteers

A wealthy philanthropist and social reformer, Gerrit Smith was one of the "Secret Six" who gave financial backing to the Harpers Ferry raid. When he learned that the raid had failed, he suffered a breakdown and was confined for several weeks in the insane asylum at Utica, in New York State. (Library of Congress LC-DIG-cwpbh-02632)

to be formed "army of liberation." Later, on October 10, 1859, and a week before the raid, he ordered that this army would be "divided into battalions of four companies, which would contain, when full, seventy-two men including officers in each company, or two hundred and eighty-eight in the battalion. Each company was to be divided into 'bands' of seven men under a corporal, and every two 'bands' made a 'section' under a sergeant."

Although Brown was ready to implement his raid on Harpers Ferry after the Chatham Convention, having scheduled the symbolic date July 4, 1858 to act, the activities of Hugh Forbes forced him to delay. Distressed by what Forbes might know and divulge to others, the "Secret Six" were anxious to postpone Brown's undertaking and advised him to return west in order to again draw attention to himself as a continuing part of Kansas affairs. Adopting the alias "Shubel Morgan," Brown re-established his small "army" in Kansas near the Missouri border during the summer of 1858 and supervised the construction of a small stone-and-wood fortification by the Little Osage River called Bain's Fort. Following a prolonged bout of malarial fever that incapacitated him for much of the rest of the year, he crossed over the state line into Missouri toward the end of December 1858, in response to a plea to liberate some slaves. Freeing 11 slaves from three plantations near Westport, one of his men killed a slaveholder in the process, which resulted in a reward of $3,000 being offered by Governor Robert Stewart, of Missouri, for Brown's capture, while President James Buchanan promised $250 for the same outcome. According to a report in *Frederick Douglass' Paper*, published in Rochester, New York, in response to the latter, "old Captain Brown" issued a proclamation offering "two dollars and fifty cents for Mr. Buchanan's head."

With much of eastern Kansas in a state of alarm, the fugitive abolitionist led the liberated blacks, plus a baby born along the way, more than 1,000 miles from Kansas to Detroit, Michigan, where the fugitives crossed into Canada and safety during March 1859. Traveling east through Ohio, Brown next gave several fund-raising lectures about his Kansas exploits in Cleveland and Jefferson. Arriving back in New England he contacted members of the "Secret Six" and found Gerrit Smith, George Stearns, and Frank Sanborn still firmly supportive of his plans. However, support from Samuel Howe and Thomas Higginson had waned, while Theodore Parker was dying of tuberculosis in Europe. Despite some disapproval of his Missouri raid, Brown still managed to receive enough money to arrange for the completion of his order for pikes from Charles Blair originally placed in March 1857. He also arranged for the transfer to Chambersburg, Pennsylvania, of weapons stored in Ohio. At the same time, black female abolitionist Harriet Tubman suggested July 4, 1859 to both John Brown and Gerrit Smith as "a good time to 'raise the mill,'" or put plans in place for the raid. On the same date, Brown rented the farm of the late Dr. Booth Kennedy, which was in Maryland about seven miles northeast of Harpers Ferry, to use as his base of operations.

Assuming the name "Isaac Smith," John Brown arrived at Harpers Ferry with his sons Owen and Oliver. It is not known if they made contact with

John Cook, who had been living in the community for about a year. Meanwhile, second-in-command John Kagi took up residence at Chambersburg, Pennsylvania, under the alias "John Henrie," to receive and forward weapons and supplies for what he stated was a proposed "filibustering expedition" to conquer territory and spread slavery in Central America. Brown was soon joined by Watson Brown and William and Dauphin Thompson, who arrived on August 6. Osborne Anderson, John Copeland, Barclay and Edwin Coppoc, Albert Hazlett, Lewis Leary, William Leeman, Francis Merriam, Dangerfield Newby, Aaron Stevens, Stewart Taylor, and Charles P. Tidd arrived between early August and mid-October 1859. Called his "band of shepherds" by John Brown, this group also referred to themselves as "surveyors." To avoid arousing suspicion in the neighborhood, Brown arranged for several female members of his family to join them, and daughter Annie and daughter-in-law Martha, the wife of Oliver, arrived during the latter part of July and remained until the end of September, cooking and cleaning for the growing number of men at the Kennedy farm. Spending most of the daylight hours out of sight in the barn and farmhouse attic, the men passed the time writing letters and studying Hugh Forbes' military manual. Sometimes they underwent "a quiet, though rigid drill" led by Aaron Stevens, the only raider with any regular military experience, having enlisted in the 1st US Dragoons after Mexican War service. Finding confinement especially difficult, Albert Hazlett and William Leeman would wander out in the woods and even visited John Cook in Harpers Ferry on occasions.

As this small force gathered, their leader had one more person he wished to convince to fight at his side. On September 12 he and John Kagi slipped away from the farm to meet once again with Frederick Douglass at an old stone quarry near Chambersburg, Pennsylvania. Of this meeting Douglass, who was accompanied by a runaway slave called "Emperor," also known as Shields Green, recorded: "The taking of Harpers Ferry, of which Captain Brown had merely hinted before, was now declared as his settled purpose, and he wanted to know what I thought of it. I at once opposed the measure with all the arguments at my command. To me such a measure would be fatal to running off slaves [which was the original plan] ... and fatal to all engaged in doing so. It would be an attack upon the Federal government, and would array the whole country against us." He added that, as Harpers Ferry was surrounded on all sides by commanding heights, it was "a perfect steel-trap," and that the raiders would "never get out alive." In response, Brown gave the impression that he cared little that his plan might fail. It seemed as if he accepted that failure with its ensuing martyrdom would do more to achieve his ultimate goal than any "success" might have done. He did not "at all object to rousing the nation; it seemed to him that something startling was just what the nation needed."

When the black abolitionist refused to join him, Brown continued, "'Come with me, Douglass; I will defend you with my life. I want you for a special purpose. When I strike, the bees will begin to swarm, and I shall want you to help hive them.' When about to leave I asked Green what he had

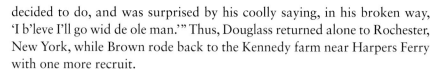

Brown's men prepare to attack Harpers Ferry

According to black abolitionist leader Frederick Douglass, the soul of John Brown had been "pierced with the iron of slavery." He disapproved of Brown's plan to start an armed slave rebellion in the South. (Library of Congress LC-USZ62-15887)

decided to do, and was surprised by his coolly saying, in his broken way, 'I b'leve I'll go wid de ole man.'" Thus, Douglass returned alone to Rochester, New York, while Brown rode back to the Kennedy farm near Harpers Ferry with one more recruit.

On Sunday, October 16, 1859, John Brown gathered his small army together for prayers, following which he read out the Constitution formulated at Chatham as some of his new recruits had not heard it before. Additional oaths were sworn, and a series of 11 orders were issued concerning the mission, the essence of which was to seize the arms at the Federal Armory and Arsenal, plus the Hall's Rifle Works, and carry them off into the neighboring mountains, along with a number of hostages from among the wealthier slave-holding citizens of the vicinity, who would be held until they agreed to free their slaves.

The assault party was to make as little noise as possible as they marched to Harpers Ferry. As the approach was made, Charles Tidd and John Cook were to tear down the telegraph wires along the railroad on the Maryland side of the Potomac River, and would repeat the same destruction on the Virginia side after the town had been captured. John Kagi and Aaron Stevens were to cross the Baltimore and Ohio Railroad bridge first to capture the watchman and detain him until the fire engine house in the Armory grounds was secured as a headquarters. The others would then cross, with John Brown riding in a one-horse covered wagon and the others walking in pairs behind "some distance apart." Once the whole party had crossed over,

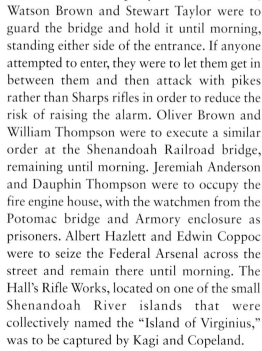

Watson Brown and Stewart Taylor were to guard the bridge and hold it until morning, standing either side of the entrance. If anyone attempted to enter, they were to let them get in between them and then attack with pikes rather than Sharps rifles in order to reduce the risk of raising the alarm. Oliver Brown and William Thompson were to execute a similar order at the Shenandoah Railroad bridge, remaining until morning. Jeremiah Anderson and Dauphin Thompson were to occupy the fire engine house, with the watchmen from the Potomac bridge and Armory enclosure as prisoners. Albert Hazlett and Edwin Coppoc were to seize the Federal Arsenal across the street and remain there until morning. The Hall's Rifle Works, located on one of the small Shenandoah River islands that were collectively named the "Island of Virginius," was to be captured by Kagi and Copeland.

A few days prior to the raid, Cook had traveled west along the Charleston turnpike secretly collecting statistics on the population of slaves and the names of their masters in order to select candidates for hostage-taking during the raid. Among the latter whose acquaintance he made was Lewis W. Washington, a colonel on the staff of Henry A. Wise, Governor of Virginia, and great grandnephew of President George Washington. Receiving Cook politely, Colonel Washington showed him a sword reputed to have been sent to George Washington in 1780 by Frederick the Great accompanied by a verbal message, "From the oldest General in the World to the Greatest," plus a pair of pistols reportedly used by the Marquis de Lafayette during the Revolutionary War and presented to George Washington as a personal souvenir. Lewis Washington became an obvious choice as a hostage and his historic weaponry would lend special significance to events if commandeered and used during the raid. According to Brown, Osborne Anderson being "a colored man, and colored men being only things in the South, it is proper that the South be taught a lesson upon this point," and so he would be given the responsibility of seizing the weapons. Slaveholder Thomas Alstadt was also selected by Cook as a likely hostage during the same trip.

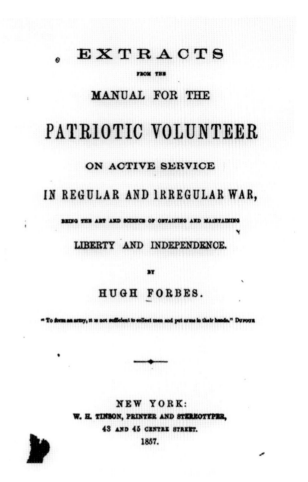

> EXTRACTS
>
> FROM THE
>
> MANUAL FOR THE
>
> # PATRIOTIC VOLUNTEER
>
> ON ACTIVE SERVICE
>
> IN REGULAR AND IRREGULAR WAR,
>
> BEING THE ART AND SCIENCE OF OBTAINING AND MAINTAINING
>
> LIBERTY AND INDEPENDENCE.
>
> BY
>
> HUGH FORBES.
>
> " To form an army, it is not sufficient to collect men and put arms in their hands." DUFOUR
>
> NEW YORK:
> W. H. TINSON, PRINTER AND STEREOTYPER,
> 43 AND 45 CENTRE STREET.
> 1857.

Back at Harpers Ferry, Cook and others, with the help of freed blacks, would take all available wagons to the Kennedy farmhouse to collect the pikes guarded by Owen Brown, Frank Merriam, and Barclay Coppoc, which would be carried to an unoccupied log cabin sometimes used as a school house in the mountain on the Maryland side of the Potomac about three-quarters of a mile from the entrance to the bridge. These weapons would be waiting for the raiders in the event that the slave revolt failed and they had to fall back into Maryland. But if all went to plan and the anticipated slave revolt spread, the raiders were to escape into the mountains with growing numbers of freed blacks and liberated weapons, setting fire to the buildings and bridges at Harpers Ferry as they departed using "tow balls steeped in oil," believed to have been made by Annie and Isabel Brown before they left the Kennedy farm. Although the latter articles were probably taken to Harpers Ferry in the wagon, the raiders did not have the opportunity to use them.

It was the original intention of John Brown to launch his raid on Harpers Ferry on the night of October 24, 1859, but because a local woman had spotted black men at the Kennedy farm, and he thought his intentions might be exposed, he ordered the attack to go ahead on October 16. This last minute change of plan was to have disastrous consequences on the outcome

The military treatise by British mercenary Hugh Forbes entitled *Manual for the Patriotic Volunteer; On Active Service in Regular and Irregular War; Being the Art and Science of Obtaining and Maintaining Liberty and Independence*, had a great influence on John Brown during the preparation for his raid on Harpers Ferry. This edition was published in 1857. It is open to speculation how much notice he took of the quote below the title by Swiss military strategist Guillaume-Henri Dufour: "To form an army, it is not sufficient to collect men and put arms in their hands." (Author's collection)

The raiders stored pikes and other weapons in an unoccupied log cabin sometimes used as a schoolhouse on the Maryland side of the Potomac River about three-quarters of a mile from the entrance to the Baltimore and Ohio Railroad bridge. (Anne S. K. Brown Military Collection)

of the operation as, according to Redpath, other volunteers in "Canada, Kansas, New England, and the neighboring Free States" intent on being involved were unable to do so on this earlier date. Abolitionist Richard Hinton was in nearby Chambersburg at "a black operated underground railroad post" awaiting word to join Brown, while Harriet Tubman was trying to raise recruits for the venture elsewhere. Convinced that he had sufficient numbers to achieve his objective, Brown waited until after nightfall on October 16, 1859, and issued the fateful order, "Men, get on your arms; we will proceed to the Ferry."

THE RAIDERS

The "Provisional Army" commanded by John Brown consisted of 22 men including himself. Of these, 16 were white and five were of African American descent. Most of the former were commissioned as "officers," with Aaron Stevens, John H. Kagi, John E. Cook, Charles Tidd, William Leeman, William Thompson, Jeremiah Anderson, plus Brown's three sons, Owen, Oliver, and Watson as captains, and Albert Hazlett, Edwin Coppoc, and Dauphin Thompson as lieutenants. The remaining men were "privates." At 59, Brown was the eldest of the group with freed slave Dangerfield Newby second eldest at 44. Dauphin Adolphus Thompson was the youngest at 20, although Oliver Brown, Barclay Coppoc and William Leeman were born in the same year but were a few weeks older. The average age of the 21 volunteers was 25 years and five months. Only one was of foreign birth, while the rest were considered old American stock.

Of Swiss descent, **John H. Kagi** (listed as Kagy in the 1850 census) was born at Bristolville in Trumbull County, Ohio, on March 15, 1835. Self-educated, he taught school at Hawkinstown in Shenandoah County, Virginia, during the early 1850s but being opposed to slavery was forced to return to Ohio, following which he became a confirmed abolitionist. He arrived in Kansas Territory in 1856 as a member of the Jayhawkers, or Free-State guerrillas, led by James H. Lane, and also became the Kansas correspondent for various newspapers including the *Tribune* and *Evening Post*, of New York, and *National Era* of Washington, DC. Enlisting in Co. B, 2nd Regiment of Free-State Volunteers, commanded by future fellow raider Aaron D. Stevens, who was also known as Colonel Charles Whipple, he was captured by US troops and imprisoned first at Lecompton and then at Tecumseh. However, when eventually liberated on January 30, 1857, he was involved in an altercation with pro-slavery lawyer Rush Elmore in which both men sustained wounds. According to a report in the *National Era*, possibly written anonymously by himself, Kagi's life was saved when a bullet that struck him over the heart was stopped by a memorandum book in his

Commissioned a "captain" in John Brown's "Provisional Army," John H. Kagi was killed while attempting to escape from the Hall's Rifle Works on October 17, 1859, after the Harpers Ferry raid had failed. (Kansas State Historical Society)

pocket. Again arrested for his part in the affray, he was released on bail of $3,000, and returned to Ohio to recover from his wounds. Upon return to Kansas later that year he became John Brown's chief confidant, assistant and "adjutant general," and was given the title of "Secretary of War" in his provisional government on May 10, 1858.

Born into a wealthy family at Haddam, Connecticut, in 1829, **John E. Cook** was a former student at Yale and brother-in-law of Ashbel P. Willard, governor of Indiana. He studied law at William and Mary College in Virginia, and taught in several public schools whilst still a teenager. He served unsuccessfully as a clerk in the office of New York lawyer Ogden Hoffman from 1854 through 1855, and arrived in Kansas in June 1856, just after the battle of Black Jack. Reputed to be an excellent marksman, he was commissioned a captain in Brown's "Provisional Army" in May 1858, and shortly afterward volunteered to conduct a prolonged reconnaissance of Harpers Ferry and surrounding country. Arriving in Virginia in early June, he stayed at Martinsburg, boarding with Mrs. Kennedy, whose daughter Mary he married soon after. He taught district school, and also gave writing lessons. He peddled maps and traveled as a book agent in the Valley of Virginia. For some time he also operated the canal lock at the north end of the US Armory grounds. He was often in the Armory gathering information and made the acquaintance of local plantation owner Lewis Washington, great grandnephew of George Washington, and formulated the plan to take him as a hostage, while seizing a sword and pistols once owned by the first President. Advocating a raid on Harpers Ferry, he wanted to burn the buildings and railroad bridges, and carry off such US arms as their means of transportation would permit.

Charles Plummer Tidd was born in Palermo, Waldo County, Maine, on New Year's Day, 1834. Described as a "woodsman," he migrated to Kansas

JOHN BROWN AND MEMBERS OF HIS "PROVISIONAL ARMY"

Our plate is based on contemporary accounts of **John Brown** and his followers in October, 1859. During an interview in 1881 Benjamin Mills, Master of the Harpers Ferry Armory at the time of the raid, described Brown as "an old looking man, fifty nine years of age" who "stood about, five feet nine or ten inches. He had no teeth, and his hair was rather long. He had a piercing hazel eye, and the whole countenance was expressive of great determination. He was rather thin and slender of build, with quite long legs. He stooped forward from the hips while walking. He wore a heavy [white] beard; dressing in a light colored frock coat. An otter skin cap adorned his head..." He is shown armed with the captured sword reputed to have been gifted by Frederick the Great to President George Washington in 1780. He also carries a pistol used by the Marquis de Lafayette

during the Revolutionary War and presented to Washington as a personal souvenir.

Of mixed race, **John A. Copeland, Jr.** appears as several of the raiders were described, with a blanket draped over his shoulders for additional warmth. When finally captured on October 25, 1859, **John E. Cook** was described as wearing "a black slouch hat, high crown; a somewhat faded black frock coat, with outside pockets; light brown pants; very large, heavy boots, and a red and white striped calico shirt." He had "a sallow complexion, light hair, cut straight across behind; light, sandy beard and moustache, neither heavy." His general appearance was "very rough and shabby." Both the latter two men are armed with Sharps rifles and bowie knifes.

One of John Brown's "officers," William Thompson was captured while attempting to negotiate with armed citizens under a flag of truce. After being shot in the head, his body was thrown into the Potomac. (Kansas State Historical Society)

with the second party of Dr. Calvin Cutter, of Worcester, Massachusetts, in 1856. He joined John Brown's "army" at Tabor, Iowa, in 1857. Thereafter, he became one of Brown's closest associates, and returned to Kansas with him in 1858 when he took part in the raid into Missouri.

One of the youngest members of Brown's "army," **William H. Leeman** was born in Newcastle, Lincoln County, Maine, on March 20, 1839. Educated in the public schools at Saco and Hallowell, Maine, he was working in a shoe factory at Haverhill, Massachusetts, at the age of 14. In 1856 he attempted to join the Free-State forces in Kansas as a member of the first Cutter party from Worcester, Massachusetts. When the route of this group was blocked by pro-slavery forces at Lexington, Missouri, he traveled up the Mississippi River from St. Louis to Davenport, Iowa, following which he had found his way to Tabor by September 9, 1856, where he joined John Brown's "Volunteer Regulars."

Both **William** and **Dauphin Adolphus Thompson** were the sons of farmer Roswell Thompson, a neighbor of John Brown at North Elba, New York. Born with his twin brother Willard in August 1833, William Thompson left the Adirondacks and joined Brown in Kansas after his elder brother Henry had been severely wounded during the fighting at Black Jack. His brother Dauphin joined him shortly afterward. Being born on April 17, 1838, he became the youngest member of Brown's followers. Their brother Henry had married John Brown's daughter Ruth, while their youngest sister Isabel married Watson Brown.

The grandson of Virginia slaveholders, **Jeremiah Anderson** was born in Indiana on April 17, 1833. After attending school at Galesburg, Illinois, and Kossuth, Iowa, he worked as a farmhand, peddler, and employee at a sawmill before migrating to Kansas in August 1857 where he settled by the Little Osage River, Bourbon County, about a mile from Bain's Fort. Serving as a lieutenant in Captain James Montgomery's "Self-Protective Company" of Jayhawkers, he was twice arrested by pro-slavery forces and imprisoned for ten weeks at Fort Scott. During April 1858 he was involved in an attack on a troop of the 1st US Cavalry sent to enforce Federal authority in the territory, and was with John Brown on the slave raid into Missouri that December, after which he continued to follow Brown's fortunes. Of his determination to continue the fight for freedom, he wrote on July 5, 1859: "lions of fellow-beings require it of us; their cries for help go out to the universe daily and hourly. Whose is it to help them? Is it yours? Is it mine? It is every man's… But there are a few who dare to answer this call and dare to answer it in a manner that will make this land of liberty and equality shake to the center."

Named after his grandfather and born on November 4, 1824, at Hudson, Ohio, **Owen Brown** was John Brown's third son, and his stalwart, reliable lieutenant both in Kansas and later at Harpers Ferry. Both **Watson** and **Oliver Brown** were born in Franklin, Ohio, on October 7, 1835 and March

9, 1839 respectively. Oliver was in Kansas with his father from June until October 1856, and received his "baptism of fire" at Black Jack.

Migrating to southern Kansas in early 1857, 19-year-old Pennsylvanian **Albert Hazlett**, alias Edward, alias William Harrison, also joined the Jayhawkers under James Montgomery before meeting up with John Brown during the latter part of 1858. He took part in the Missouri slave raid and was with Brown when he led the rescued slaves to Canada. Prior to the Harpers Ferry raid he worked on his brother's farm at Indiana in western Pennsylvania, joining the others at Kennedy farm in the early part of September 1859.

The childhood of **Edwin** and **Barclay Coppoc** alias **Coppic** was disrupted when their father died in 1841. Six-year-old Edwin lived for the next nine years with the family of John Butler, a farmer, near Salem, Ohio, following which he moved with his mother to Springdale, Iowa, while three-year-old Barclay was raised by the family of farmer William Fisher of Perry, Ohio. At 23 years of age, Edwin settled in Kansas in the spring of 1858 but took no part in the troubles, returning to Springdale later that year. He and his younger brother Barclay joined John Brown when he passed through Iowa en route for Canada with the rescued slaves in early 1859.

Born into a wealthy abolitionist family at Framingham, Massachusetts, on November 17, 1837, **Francis J. Merriam** joined John Brown after his arrival in Kansas in 1858 despite his frailty and blindness in one eye. Coming from old Puritan stock, the great-grandfather of **Aaron D. Stevens** had been a captain in the Revolutionary army. Born in Lisbon, New London County, Connecticut, on March 15, 1831, Stevens ran away from home in 1847 at 16 years of age and enlisted in the 1st Massachusetts Regiment, in which he served during the Mexican–American War. At the close of that conflict he enlisted in the 1st US Dragoons and was tried for mutiny having been involved in a drunken riot at Taos, New Mexico, in 1855 during which he assaulted the regimental major. Although given the death penalty, his sentence was commuted by President Franklin Pierce to three years hard

Free black raider Osborne Anderson managed to escape from Harpers Ferry after the raid failed. Resuming his career in Canada as a writer, he wrote *A Voice from Harper's Ferry*, which was published in Boston, Massachusetts, in 1861. (Kansas State Historical Society)

10.30PM, OCTOBER 16

The raiders cross the bridge into Harpers Ferry and begin seizing key points

labor at Fort Leavenworth, from which post he escaped on January 2, 1856 to join the Kansas Free State forces. Assuming the name "Charles Whipple," he became colonel of the 2nd Kansas Militia, and on August 7, 1856 joined John Brown's "army of liberation."

The only raider not of American birth, 23-year-old **Stewart Taylor** was born in Uxbridge, north of Toronto, in Canada. A spiritualist, student of history, and ardent abolitionist, he was a wagon-maker by trade. Taylor migrated to Iowa in 1858 where he became acquainted with John Brown and attended the Chatham Convention. After that body adjourned, he found employment in Illinois until John Kagi contacted him early in July 1859, at which point he hastened to the Kennedy Farm fearful that he may have been too late to take part in the raid.

Both **Lewis S. Leary** and **John A. Copeland, Jr** were free blacks associated with Oberlin College in Ohio. Of mixed race, Leary was descended from Irishman Jeremiah O'Leary who fought in the Revolutionary War under General Nathanael Greene, while his mother was part African and part Croatoan, or Native American, from North Carolina. (The Croatoan people are believed by many to have absorbed the "lost colonists" or English settlers, left behind on Roanoke Island by Captain John White in 1587.) Like his father, Leary was a saddler and harness-maker at Fayetteville, North Carolina. In 1857 he moved to Oberlin and met John Brown in Cleveland. Born at Raleigh, North Carolina, on August 15, 1834, **John A. Copeland, Jr** became a carpenter and moved with his family to Oberlin in 1842. He was for some time a student in the preparatory department of Oberlin College, and was enlisted in John Brown's gathering force with Lewis S. Leary during September 1859. Earlier in 1858 both Leary and Copeland had been among 37 men involved in the rescue of John Price, a fugitive slave from Kentucky who had been captured and held by authorities under the 1850 Fugitive Slave Act. Both were jailed in Cleveland until July 1859. (Leary was an uncle of Copeland.)

Also a free black, **Osborne P. Anderson** was born at West Fallowfield, Pennsylvania, on July 27, 1830. A printer by trade, he worked for the *Provincial Freeman* newspaper at Chatham, Canada West, where he first met John Brown in 1858. A fugitive slave from Charleston, South Carolina, **Shields Green** or "Emperor" found freedom in Canada. Working as a servant and clothes cleaner in Rochester, New York, he met Frederick Douglass who introduced him to John Brown in August 1859. Twenty-three-year-old **Dangerfield Newby** was born into slavery in the Shenandoah Valley, Virginia, in 1815, and was freed by his white Scottish father. Newby was unable to purchase the freedom of his wife and seven children as their master Jesse Jennings raised the price after the freed black had saved the $1,500 previously agreed upon for their manumission. As a result, he hoped to free them by force starting with the raid on Harpers Ferry in October 1859.

THE RAID

The raiders met no one as they proceeded in the dim moonlight for about one and a half hours through a chill October night towards Harpers Ferry. According to Osborne Anderson, they marched along "as solemnly as a funeral procession," with John Brown riding in a wagon that carried some of the pikes to be distributed among the freed slaves. Entering the Maryland side of the covered Baltimore and Ohio Railroad bridge at about 10.30pm, the raiders carried out a previously arranged order and fastened their accoutrements, including cartridge boxes containing 40 rounds, on the outside of their clothing. John Kagi and Aaron Stevens were first to cross the bridge. Their approach was so quiet that they took Bill Williams, the unarmed watchman, completely by surprise. Once Williams had been captured, the other raiders crossed over. Still riding in the wagon, Brown ordered Stewart Taylor and his son Watson to seize and guard the Shenandoah bridge while he led the others to the gates of the nearby US Armory, which they forced open with a crowbar despite the protests of watchman Daniel Whelan who refused to hand over the keys. "One fellow," recalled Whelan, "took me; they all gathered about me and looked in my face; I was nearly scared to death for so many guns about; I did not know the minute or the hour I should drop; they told me to be very quiet and still and make no noise or else they would put me to eternity. After that, the head man of them, Brown, said to me: 'I came here from Kansas, and this is a slave State. I want to free all the negroes in this State; I have possession now of the United States armory, and if the citizens interfere with me I must only burn the town and have blood.'"

John Brown next seized as his headquarters the fire engine house, which was the first building on the left inside the Armory gates. The two prisoners were left there under the charge of Jeremiah Anderson and Dauphin Thompson. Albert Hazlett and Edwin Coppoc were next sent across the street to take possession of the US Arsenal buildings, which stood unguarded in a separate enclosure, while William Thompson and Oliver Brown seized the Shenandoah toll bridge. Kagi and Copeland proceeded farther along

Shenandoah Street to occupy the Hall's Rifle Works. According to his account of events, Osborne Anderson also accompanied them. "When we went there," he wrote, "we told the watchman who was outside of the building our business, and asked him to go along with us, as we had come to take possession of the town, and make use of the Armory in carrying out our object. He obeyed the command without hesitation." Thus by 11pm on October 16, 1859, all the key points in Harpers Ferry had been captured and everything appeared to be going according to plan.

At midnight the relief watchman, an Irishman named Patrick Higgins, came on duty at the Maryland end of the railroad bridge. Perturbed when he noticed that the lanterns at both ends of the bridge were extinguished, he still waited to punch the time clock which he and Williams were required to do every 30 minutes on the hour and half hour by railroad regulations. He then found that Williams had last punched in at 10.30pm. With lantern in hand, he walked nervously over the bridge looking for him. As he approached the Harpers Ferry side he was accosted by two men who stepped out of the shadows and ordered him to halt. Higgins later commented, "I didn't know what 'Halt' mint [sic] then any more than a hog knows about a holiday." Attempting to ignore them, his arm was grabbed by Watson Brown, but he struck his assailant across the head and ran on to seek refuge in the Wager House Hotel. As he made his escape Stewart Taylor took aim and fired the first shot of the raid which went straight through Higgins' hat and grazed his scalp. Thus, the alarm began to spread as, awakened by the gunshot and Higgins' noisy arrival, the hotel staff and guests peered nervously out of their windows. Living in rooms opposite the hotel, local physician Dr. John D. Starry went to his window and later testified that he saw "two armed men passing from the bridge towards the armory gate. These men were low fellows." Overcome with curiosity, the barkeep at the hotel ventured out soon after and was captured. John Brown exchanged him in the morning for breakfast for 40 men which number included his prisoners and hostages.

With everything apparently still going well, all the raiders without a specific duty reported back at the engine house, at which point John Brown ordered Stevens, Cook, Tidd, Leary, Shields Green, and Osborne Anderson "to the country" to capture hostages. Of the journey out of Harpers Ferry, Anderson wrote: "On the road, we met some colored men, to whom we made known our purpose, when they immediately agreed to join us. They said they had been long waiting for an opportunity of the kind. Stevens then asked them to go around among the colored people and circulate the news, when each started off in a different direction. The result was that many colored men gathered to the scene of action." At about 1.30am the raiders arrived at "Beall-Air," the farm of Lewis Washington, at Halltown, about four miles west of Harpers Ferry, where they took a greatly frightened Lewis Washington into their custody and seized his much-prized sword and pistols. Commandeering a two-horse carriage and four-horse wagon, they also rounded up four slaves and returned to Harpers Ferry via a neighboring farm, gathering another six slaves and taking Thomas Alstadt and his 18-year-old son as additional hostages.

Back at Harpers Ferry, African American porter Hayward Shepherd stepped out of the Railroad Office to investigate the absence of watchmen on the bridge. According to *Harper's Weekly* artist and reporter David Hunter Strother, "When he got there he was approached by several armed men, one of whom handed him a rifle, and ordered him to stand guard in the cause of freedom. Heywood [*sic*] expostulated with them, and resolutely refused to take the rifle." Turning to go back to the office, he was shot in the back and died shortly afterward. Thus, a free black from Winchester, Virginia, became the first serious casualty of the Harpers Ferry raid. It is possible that the killing of this man did much to prevent a general insurrection among the local blacks, as some of the farmers said they noticed an unusual excitement among their slaves the day before the raid. If some of them knew of the intended attack, it is probable they were deterred from taking part when learning that one of their own people was the first fatality.

Meanwhile, the eastbound Baltimore and Ohio "Through Express" approached Harpers Ferry at 1.20am and was stopped at the upper end of the town by watchman Patrick Higgins, who had managed to evade capture. Alighting from the train, Conductor Andrew J. Phelps and Baggage Master Luther Simpson were apprised of the situation and marched over to the Armory grounds to find out what the "insurgents" wanted, to which John Brown replied, "We want liberty; the grounds, bridge, and town are in our hands." Back on the train, excited passengers had no idea why their train had been stopped, although a rumor began to spread that dissatisfied Irish laborers working on the canal north of Harpers Ferry had gone on strike and occupied the town. One passenger from New York recalled in a report in the local newspaper the *Shepherdstown Register* on October 22, 1859: "Every light in the town had been previously extinguished by the lawless mob. The train therefore remained stationary and the passengers, terribly affrighted, remained in the cars all night. The hotels were closed and no entrance could be had into them. All the streets were in possession of the men, and every road, lane and avenue leading to the town guarded or barricaded by them."

Raising the Alarm

At about 6.30am, John Brown committed his first fatal error of the raid when he advised Conductor Phelps that he had "no intention of interfering with the comfort of passengers or hindering the United States mails," and that the Through Express should continue on its way. This was an extraordinary decision considering that the success of the operation depended on his being able to capture weapons and escape into the mountains before word could spread to Washington, DC or elsewhere. Unarmed and with cool deliberation, Brown walked with Phelps across the short bridge to the north of the Armory grounds. Waiting with him until the train received the signal to proceed he strode back alone as the engine chugged across the Potomac River bridge towards Maryland Heights and eventually on to Baltimore.

According to James Redpath, the passengers threw messages out of the windows of the cars in an effort to spread news of the "insurrection" as

THE PLAN OF ATTACK

OCTOBER 16, 1859

Harpers Ferry was nestled at the foot of Maryland, Loudoun, and Bolivar Heights at the confluence of the Potomac and Shenandoah rivers. From across the Potomac on Maryland Heights on the night of October 16, 1859, the small township appeared to be a disorganized cluster of industrial buildings, hotels, saloons, shops, and private dwellings that stretched along the banks of the two rivers and climbed Bolivar Heights to its rear. Its busy railroad depot accommodated the Baltimore & Ohio and Winchester & Potomac railroads, which ran through the community along raised platforms supported by wood-and-stone pillars.

Commercial and military supplies were transported along the Chesapeake & Ohio Canal which ran along the north bank of the Potomac River. About half Harpers Ferry's population of about 2,500 people were African American, nearly all of whom were free. Most of the whites in the community were not local but skilled Northern workers who had migrated south to work at the Government Armory and Hall's Rifle Works.

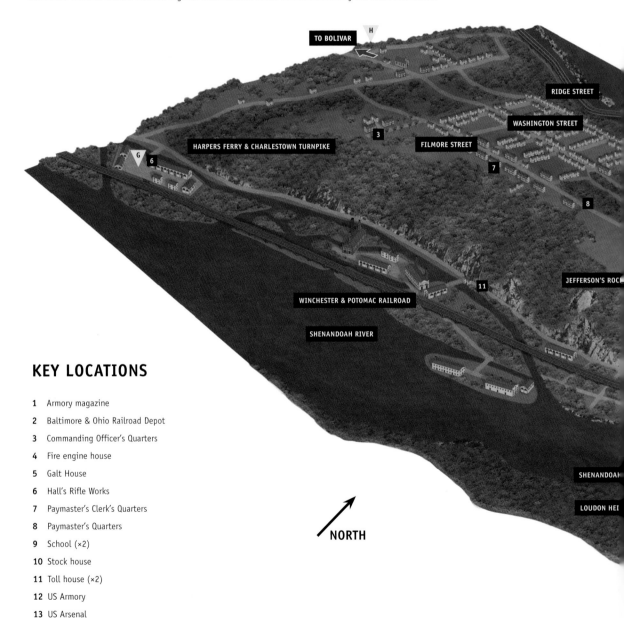

KEY LOCATIONS

1   Armory magazine

2   Baltimore & Ohio Railroad Depot

3   Commanding Officer's Quarters

4   Fire engine house

5   Galt House

6   Hall's Rifle Works

7   Paymaster's Clerk's Quarters

8   Paymaster's Quarters

9   School (×2)

10 Stock house

11 Toll house (×2)

12 US Armory

13 US Arsenal

14 Wager House Hotel

15 Water tank

▼ EVENTS

A As the raiders approach Harpers Ferry at about 10.30pm on October 16, 1859, Tidd and Cook would tear down the telegraph wires along the railroad tracks on both sides of the Baltimore & Ohio Railroad bridge. They would also lead the way across the bridge with John Brown following in a wagon and the others walking in pairs behind.

B Kagy and Stevens capture the watchman at the Harpers Ferry end of the bridge.

C Taylor and Watson Brown guard the Baltimore & Ohio Railroad Bridge.

D John Brown and the others capture the Armory, following which their prisoners would be held in the fire engine house.

E Hazlett and Edwin Coppick occupy the US Arsenal across the street.

F William Thompson and Oliver Brown seize the Shenandoah Bridge.

G Kagy and Copeland proceed along Shenandoah Street to capture the Hall's Rifle Works.

H Stevens, Cook, Tidd, Leary, Green, and Osborne Anderson march west of Harpers Ferry and capture local slaveholders.

I Helped by freed blacks, Cook, Tidd, and Leeman return to the Kennedy farmhouse with wagons to collect pikes guarded by Owen Brown, Merriam, and Barclay Coppoc. These were to be

carried to a schoolhouse on the Maryland side of the Potomac. Guarded by Cook, these were to be waiting for the raiders when they escaped back across the railroad bridge with freed slaves and liberated firearms.

J By dawn on October 17, the town was to be burned using flaming tow balls as the raiders withdrew back across the bridge and escaped into the mountains.

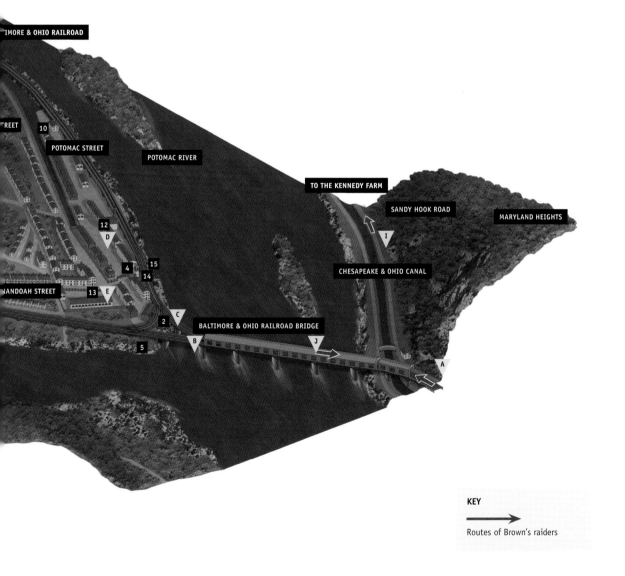

KEY

→ Routes of Brown's raiders

Photograph circa 1860, the fire engine house and guardhouse stand at left inside the gates to the grounds of the US Armory at Harpers Ferry. The iron gates over which John Brown's raiders scrambled have been removed. The Armory buildings at right consisted of brick superstructures built around cast-iron framing, and had sheet-iron or slate roofs, all erected upon heavy stone foundations. (Historic Photo Collection, Harpers Ferry National Historical Park)

the train rushed onward into Maryland. By 7.05am it had traveled 20 miles east of Harpers Ferry reaching Monocacy, from which place the telegraph wire remained intact. There Phelps ordered Dispatcher F. Mantz to telegraph William P. Smith, the Transportation Master at Baltimore, and by about 8.00am, an incredulous telegrapher at the Camden Station in Baltimore had handed the equally disbelieving Smith the first news of an attack upon the US Armory and Arsenal at Harpers Ferry. Phelps' message stated: "Express train bound east, under my charge, was stopped this morning at Harpers Ferry by armed abolitionists. They have possession of the bridge and the arms and armory of the United States. Myself and Baggage Master have been fired at, and Hayward, the colored porter, is wounded very severely, being shot through the body, the ball entering … below the left shoulder blade and coming out under the left side. The Doctor says he cannot survive. They are headed by a man who calls himself Anderson, and number about one hundred and fifty strong. They say they have come to free the slaves and intend to do it at all hazards. The leader of those men requested me to say to you that this is the last train that shall pass the bridge either East or West. If it is attempted, it will be at the peril of the lives of those having them in charge. When daylight appeared we were finally permitted to pass, after being detained from half-past one o'clock to half-past six. It has been suggested you had better notify the Secretary of War at once. The telegraph wires are cut East and West of Harpers Ferry, and this is the first station that I could send a despatch from." Phelps inaccurately named Osborne Anderson as the leader of the raiders as he saw him issuing pikes to some of the freed slaves before he departed Harpers Ferry.

Much agitated, Smith sent the following terse response to Ellicott's Mills, the next stop on Phelps' route to Baltimore: "Your despatch is evidently exaggerated and written under excitement. Why should our trains be stopped by Abolitionists, and how do you know they are such and that they number one hundred or more? What is their object? Let me know at once before we proceed to extremities."

Regardless of his misgivings concerning the accuracy of Phelps' message, Smith quickly notified John W. Garrett, president of the Baltimore and Ohio Railroad, of the alarming telegram sent from Monocacy. In order to better control the situation and prevent the spread of unnecessary alarm, Garrett quickly organized his office at the Camden Station into a command center, but events were moving much faster than anyone expected. At 10.00am Smith received a telegram from John T. Quynn, B&O Railroad Agent at Frederick, Maryland, stating, "The military here are in arms. Can I send them up to Harpers Ferry?" Word of the raid had reached that city and Colonel Edward Shriver, commanding the 16th Regiment of Maryland Militia, had several military companies already assembling and ready to move on Harpers Ferry. Soon after, Superintendent Alex Diffey of the Martinsburg Station in

A great-grandnephew of General George Washington, Colonel Lewis W. Washington was one of ten hostages John Brown took with him for bargaining purposes when he retreated into the engine house during the Harpers Ferry raid. (Library of Congress LC-USZ61-116)

Virginia telegraphed to the effect that armed men had "planted guns" on the railroad bridge at Harpers Ferry, and that a group of railroad employees at Martinsburg were arming themselves in preparation to attack the raiders. Although still hopeful of containing the situation, Garrett next learned that a telegram had been sent from Frederick to the newspaper press in Baltimore reporting "a formidable negro insurrection at Harpers Ferry" and that "an armed band of abolitionists" were in "full possession of ... the United States Arsenal." The raiders were described as consisting of "about two hundred and fifty whites and a gang of negroes fighting for their freedom" who were "determined to have liberty, or die in the attempt." Aware that such startling news would spread like wildfire in the press of other major cities, and that the idea of slave rebellion might spread throughout the south, Garrett realized that the situation was beyond his means to control and rapidly fired off a succession of telegrams to higher authorities. At 10.20am he advised Secretary of War John B. Floyd that the US Armory and bridges at Harpers Ferry were in "full possession of large bands of armed men, said to be abolitionists." He continued, "Can you authorize the government officers and military from Washington to go on our train at 3.20 this afternoon to the scene, or send us full authority for volunteers from Baltimore to act." Ten minutes later he informed President James Buchanan of the situation and emphasized, "The presence of United States troops is indispensable, for the safety of government property, and of the mails."

Garrett also informed Virginia Governor Henry A. Wise, and Major General George H. Steuart, commander of the First Light Division, Maryland Volunteer Militia, of the state of emergency. Responding rather slowly at 2.40pm, Wise requested that State Adjutant General William H.

Richardson issue orders via Garrett to Colonel John Gibson, commanding the 55th Regiment of Virginia Militia, at Charlestown, authorizing him to call out as much militia as was required to suppress the trouble. This instruction would arrive several hours after militia and volunteers under Gibson had left for Harpers Ferry. Meanwhile by 1.00pm Steuart replied that four companies of Maryland militia would be on the 4.00pm train for Harpers Ferry from Baltimore.

In anticipation of the Federal government requiring transportation for troops being sent to Harpers Ferry, Garrett instructed Smith to send a telegram to the B&O Agent in Washington ordering him to place all available rail transport at the disposal of the War Department. In the meantime, Secretary of War Floyd looked for available US Regulars and found that the closest troops were the 3rd Artillery stationed at Fortress Monroe on the James Peninsula in Virginia, which was about two days journey from Harpers Ferry. Clearly they would take too long to reach the trouble spot. Regardless, Floyd dispatched a brief telegram to Colonel William Gates, their commanding officer, ordering him to send three full companies of troops aboard a boat to Baltimore, from where they would entrain for Harpers Ferry. Still in need of a rapid response force that could deal with the emergency more quickly, the only other Regulars available were the Marines stationed in Washington, DC. Rushing over to the Navy Department, Floyd briefed Secretary of the Navy Isaac Toucey of the situation at Harpers Ferry, and was assured that Marines would immediately be made available.

At the barracks in southeast Washington, Marine Commandant Colonel John Harris was informed of the situation by Chief Clerk of the Navy Charles W. Welsh just after noon. The dispatch he received stated: "Send all available marines at Head Quarters, under charge of suitable officers, by this evening's train of cars to Harpers Ferry, to protect the public property at that place, which is endangered by riotous outbreak. The men will be furnished with a proper number of ball cartridges, ammunition and rations, and will

Viewed from the northwest, Harpers Ferry stands at the confluence of the Potomac and Shenandoah rivers in this photograph taken in 1859. The buildings of the US Armory are seen alongside the riverbank with the Baltimore and Ohio Railroad bridge beyond. Lock 33 of the Chesapeake and Ohio Canal is visible across the river to the left side of the bridge. (Historic Photo Collection, Harpers Ferry NHP)

take two howitzers and shrapnel. The Commanding officer on his arrival at Harpers Ferry, will report to the Senior Army Officer who may be there in command. Otherwise he will take such measures as in his judgment may be necessary to protect the Arsenal and other property of the United States."

With Brevet Major George H. Terrett on leave of absence, First Lieutenant Israel Greene was next in seniority and would have to lead the operation, leaving First Lieutenant Edward Jones in command of the Marine Barracks. Orderly Sergeant James McDonough would serve as second-in-command. The rest of the detachment would be made up of another orderly sergeant, plus four sergeants, three corporals, two drummers, one fifer, and 74 privates. Just before the expedition marched out of the Barracks it was joined by staff officer Major William W. Russell, paymaster of the Marine Corps, who had been ordered by Harris to accompany Greene in an advisory capacity.

The Marine detachment boarded the 3.20pm train from the Washington depot of the Baltimore and Ohio, and their departure was attended by President Buchanan who was accompanied by Secretaries Floyd and Toucey. When they reached the Relay House in Maryland, the three cars in which the Marines were traveling were transferred to the 12-car Express to Harpers Ferry. Already on board was Brigadier General Charles C. Egerton, Jr with a battalion, plus four individual companies, of Maryland Volunteer Militia. The former consisted of three companies of the City Guards, while the latter was composed of the Law Grays, Shields' Guards, Independent Grays, and Wells & McComas Rifles. The total Maryland contingent amounted to 225 officers and men. These troops were supplemented by elements of the Baltimore "roughs" who were determined to see some action. The Baltimore press reported, "One individual was armed with a long duck gun, carrying over his shoulders an immense shot pouch filled with buck shot; another had a cocked hat and military roundabout [jacket], with two horse-pistols in a belt on either side of him. Those in charge of the cars attempted to prevent some of these characters from going on board, but they seemed bent on a

6.30AM, OCTOBER 17

Brown allows the B&O "Through Express" to pass through Harpers Ferry

8.00AM, OCTOBER 17

"Through Express" conductor raises the alarm by telegram

Harpers Ferry is seen from the Maryland side of the Baltimore and Ohio Railroad bridge in this *Harper's Weekly* engraving. The US Armory is shown on the opposite bank, and the Chesapeake and Ohio Canal winds its way alongside the Potomac River. (Author's collection)

39

fight, and pleaded hard for a chance to take part in the fray, and soon filled up one of the cars." Also aboard the train was Transportation Master W. P. Smith, who had been directed by B&O President Garrett to oversee the safe passage of the troops to Harpers Ferry, plus several telegraphic operators whose messages would keep Floyd and Buchanan informed.

Back in Washington, DC, Floyd still needed someone to command the operation and remembered that, before returning to his post with the 2nd Cavalry in Texas, Lieutenant Colonel Robert E. Lee was spending a few days at Arlington, his home just across the Potomac River from Washington, DC. Thus, he wrote a note to the Chief Clerk of the War Department, Colonel William R. Drinkard, instructing him to send an order to Lee with instructions to report to him immediately. Waiting in an anteroom outside Floyd's office as the messenger took the note to Drinkard was First Lieutenant James E. B. Stuart, 1st Cavalry, who wanted to see the Secretary of War on personal business concerning a government contract for a cavalry saber attachment he had devised and patented. Quickly penning the order to Lee, Drinkard handed it to Stuart who was happy to put the purpose of his visit to one side and assume the role of "special messenger." Upon delivery of the note to Lee at Arlington, Stuart offered his services as aide-de-camp, which were promptly accepted and both officers returned quickly to Washington. Reporting to Floyd at the War Department, they were taken under escort to the White House where President Buchanan explained the events of the last few hours as best he could. He was also informed that the contingent from Fortress Monroe and the detachment from the Marine Barracks were on their way to the scene. Emphasizing that he did not know what Lee would find when he arrived at Harpers Ferry, he prepared for the worst by issuing him with a proclamation of martial law.

Heading for the Washington Depot of the B&O, Stuart stopped only to borrow a uniform coat and sword, while Lee remained in his civilian clothes. Having missed the train carrying the Marines to the Relay House, the two officers waited for a special locomotive to be brought up. At this point Lee sent a telegram ahead to Frederick, Maryland, ordering the Marines to wait for him before entering Harpers Ferry. Soon after, Engine 22 and its tender pulled into the station and Engineer G. F. Gilbert called down to Lee and Stuart, beckoning them to climb up and join him in the cab. After the bemused officers had complied, the engine sped off west at full throttle and six hours later arrived at Sandy Hook, a point several miles east of Harpers Ferry. Soon after alighting from the engine, Lee received his first reliable report regarding conditions at Harpers Ferry from Lieutenant Greene, who had been waiting anxiously for him.

Overpowered by Numbers

In Harpers Ferry, the local residents began to react with panic as they awoke on the morning of October 17, 1859, to find armed men outside their doors. According to Osborne Anderson, "Men, women and children could be seen leaving their homes in every direction; some seeking refuge among residents, and in quarters further away, others climbing up the hill-sides, and hurrying off in various directions, evidently impelled by a sudden fear, which was plainly visible in their countenances or in their movements." Several newspapers, including the *Lynchburg Daily Republican* of Virginia, reported that two boys swam across the Potomac carrying a letter from a Harpers Ferry merchant pleading for help. Actively involved in attempting to organize resistance, Dr. Starry rode over to the neighboring community of Bolivar to raise the alarm and sent messengers requesting urgent help from the militia at Charlestown, about six miles further west, and to Shepherdstown, a similar distance to the northwest. He also sent runners along the Baltimore and Ohio Railroad to stop further trains coming east into Harpers Ferry. Thus the alarm was spread.

Concerned for the safety of government property, Benjamin Mills, Master of the Armory; Armistead M. Ball, Master Machinist; and John E. P. Daingerfield, Acting Paymaster, hurried to the Armory only to be taken hostage and locked in the watch-house, which adjoined the engine house on the west end of the building. At about 5am some of the employees at the Armory who knew nothing of the events of the previous night began to arrive for work only to be taken prisoner and locked in a building farther along the compound. On seeing an armed guard at the gate, one workman named Kelly asked by what authority the raiders had taken possession of government property, to which sentinel Dangerfield Newby replied, "By the

In this salt print, three-quarter length portrait taken in 1859 by New York City photographer Martin M. Lawrence, John Brown wears the beard he grew for disguise after the plans for his raid were disclosed by Hugh Forbes during the previous year. (Library of Congress LC-DIG-ppmsca-23764)

REGULAR AND STATE FORCES ACTIVATED TO QUELL THE RAID

Regular forces
Marine detachment from the barracks in southeast Washington, DC, First Lieutenant Israel Greene, with Lieutenant Colonel Robert E. Lee, 2nd Cavalry, in overall command, plus one other Marine officer and 87 enlisted Marines, accompanied by two 12-pounder howitzers.

Three companies of the 3rd Artillery, serving as infantry, reached Fort McHenry in Baltimore, Maryland, where they were halted and ordered to return to Fortress Monroe, in Virginia.

State forces: Virginia
Companies arriving at Harpers Ferry on October 17–18, 1859:

Jefferson Guards, 55th Regiment Virginia Militia, Captain John W. Rowan.

Hamtramck Guards, 31st Regiment Virginia Militia, Captain Vincent M. Butler.

Shepherdstown Troop, 31st Regiment Virginia Militia, Captain Jacob Reinhart.

Morgan Continental Guard, 31st Regiment Virginia Militia, Captain Burwell B. Washington.

Company F, 1st Regiment Virginia Militia, Captain R. Milton Cary, 60 men, accompanied by Governor Henry A. Wise.

Alexandria Rifles, 6th Battalion Virginia Militia, Captain Morton Marye, 28 men.

Companies also activated on October 18, 1859, but ordered to return to Richmond after reaching the Relay House in Maryland:

1st Regiment Virginia Militia

Richmond Grays, Captain Wyatt M. Elliott

Montgomery Guard, Captain Patrick T. Moore

Richmond Light Infantry Blues, Lieutenant William L. Maule

Virginia Rifles, Captain Albert Lybrook

Young Guard, Co. B, 179th Regiment Virginia Militia, Captain Rady

Fredericksburg Guard, Captain Joseph W. Sener

State forces: Maryland

Companies arriving from Frederick:

United Guards, Captain John T. Sinn

Junior Defenders, Captain John Ritchie

Independent Riflemen, Captain Ulysses Hobbs

Companies from Baltimore:

Law Grays, 5th Regiment Maryland Militia, Lieutenant J.C. Brown

Shields' Guards, 5th Regiment Maryland Militia, Captain Chaisty

Wells and McComas Rifles, 1st Rifle Regiment, Maryland Militia, Captain George W. Comas

Independent Grays, 53rd Regiment Maryland Militia, Lieutenant Simpson

City Guards Battalion (three companies), Major Joseph P. Warner

REGULARS AND MILITIA AT HARPERS FERRY

The **Marine corporal** wears the fatigue uniform adopted in 1839 which consisted of a sky blue kersey jacket and trousers, with rank denoted by a single half chevron of yellow worsted lace on each sleeve below the elbow. Headgear consists of a dark blue cap with stiffened top and brass letters "USM" at front. He is armed with a Model 1842 US Musket, and white buff leather belts support his black leather accoutrements. Serving as aide de camp to Robert E. Lee, **First Lieutenant J. E. B. Stuart** wears a uniform coat he borrowed before he left Washington, DC for Harpers

Ferry. According to Lieutenant Israel Greene, his hat was "very similar to the famous chapeau which he wore throughout the [Civil] war." The rest of his clothing was of civilian origin. He is armed with a Model 1840 Cavalry Officer's saber. The enlisted man of the **Jefferson Guards** wears a dark blue pattern 1851 frock with scarlet cord trim on collar and cuffs. Trousers are plain sky blue. Headgear consists of a Hardee hat with scarlet hat cord, and gold metal wreath attached to front of the crown with letters "J G" inset. He is also armed with a M1842 Musket.

authority of God Almighty." When ordered to enter as a prisoner, Kelly turned and made his escape, receiving a ball through his hat as he ran. Witnessing the incident, Irish-born grocer Thomas Boerly ran out of his shop at the corner of High and Shenandoah streets and fired his revolver at Newby but missed his mark. The next moment Boerly was shot dead by a bullet from the black raider's Sharps rifle.

By this time John Brown was, according to Osborne Anderson, "all activity" although at times he appeared "somewhat puzzled." He ordered Anderson to distribute pikes among the freed slaves who had gathered in the Armory. Among those who eagerly accepted the weapons were several farmhands who had arrived after hearing reports of the rebellion, plus Jim, a slave owned by Lewis Washington, who proved to be one of the bravest of the new recruits and, according to an eyewitness, "fought like a tiger." According to hostage John Alstadt, the raiders "armed the negroes with spears, and they would occasionally walk in to the stove [in the watch-house] … though the most of them were placed in the engine-house."

Brown next ordered Lewis Leary, plus four freed slaves and a local free man, to join Kagi and Copeland at the rifle factory. He also instructed Cook, Tidd and Leeman, with more freed slaves, to take Colonel Washington's four-horse wagon and bring more pikes from the Kennedy farm where Owen Brown, Frank Merriam, and Barclay Coppoc waited. These pikes were to be left under the care of Cook and one freed slave in a small schoolhouse near the Maryland entrance to the B&O Railroad bridge. En route to the Kennedy farm, this group took farmer Terence Byrne hostage and demanded the release of his slaves while Tidd went on to collect the pikes. Failing to find any of Byrne's three slaves, Cook and Leeman waited for Tidd to return with the laden wagon, following which they lumbered back towards Harpers Ferry. Depositing Cook at the schoolhouse with the pikes, Tidd and Leeman crossed the bridge in the wagon with the captive Byrne who was deposited in the watch-house with the other hostages. Of these movements Dr. Starry recalled: "About five minutes after five o'clock, I saw a four-horse team driving over the Baltimore and Ohio railroad bridge. I did not know whose it was. In that wagon there were three men standing up in the front part, with spears in their hands, white men, and two were walking alongside, armed with rifles."

In the meantime, some of the local menfolk in Harpers Ferry and Bolivar attempted to defend themselves and their community. One eyewitness recalled: "Very few of our citizens had arms of any sort, and what few they had were fowling pieces, and those who had them had neither powder nor shot – bullets were out of the question – so that our town, for the time being, was at the mercy of the insurgents. The arms, and what little ammunition the government had at this place, were in the hands of the enemy." However, two Armory employees, blacksmith John McClelland and machinist William D. Copeland, managed to gain access unseen by the raiders to one of the buildings in the Armory enclosure. There they acquired two single ball bullet molds, plus "all the percussion caps in that department." They next proceeded to a building outside, but contiguous to, the Armory grounds called the stock house, to which arms had been removed several weeks before for protection from flood damage when high water threatened to overflow the riverbanks. According to another eyewitness, Presbyterian minister Charles White, "The insurgents supposed they had all the guns – but the men of Bolivar … knew of the stock house guns." Sufficient powder was also secreted out of the Powder House, which stood about 100 yards to the west of the Armory, and the citizens began to arm, although it would take several hours to cast a sufficient number of musket balls. In his recollections of the raid, farmer Alexander Boteler stated, "after using up the limited supply of lead found in the village stores, pewter plates and spoons had to be melted and molded into bullets for the occasion." By 9am a number of indifferently armed citizens assembled on Camp Hill, overlooking the Potomac River to the north of Harpers Ferry, and decided that a small group of about six men should cross the Potomac River a short distance above the Ferry, and advance down the towpath of the Chesapeake and Ohio Canal to attack the raiders guarding the railroad bridge. This advance party did much to pin down Watson Brown and Stewart Taylor until reinforcements arrived.

Meanwhile, news of the insurrection reached Charlestown and by 10am Colonel John T. Gibson, of the 55th Regiment of Virginia Militia, had ordered out the blue-coated Jefferson Guards, plus a number of "the citizens of Charlestown." Joined by Robert W. Baylor, colonel of the 3rd Regiment of Cavalry, Virginia Militia, who assumed command, about 100 men traveled via railroad to Halltown where exaggerated reports were received regarding the number of insurgents in possession of Harpers Ferry. As a result, Baylor instructed the conductor aboard the train to return to Winchester and send a message to Colonel Lewis T. Moore, commander of the 31st Virginia Militia, to send the Hamtramck Guards and Shepherdstown Troop to reinforce him immediately. Continuing on foot, Baylor's command arrived at Harpers Ferry at about 11.30am, where they found the local population in "very great excitement."

Arriving at Camp Hill overlooking Harpers Ferry, Baylor ordered the Jefferson Guards, under Captain John W. Rowan, to cross the Potomac in boats about one mile above the town, following which they marched down the towpath on the Maryland side of the river to join the small group of armed citizens firing at the raiders on the railroad bridge. Baylor next formed other armed citizens into two companies and placed them under the

Anxious to avoid the possibility of widespread slave revolt following news of the raid on Harpers Ferry, pro-Southern President James Buchanan ordered a detachment of Marines to the trouble spot on October 17, 1859. (Library of Congress LC-BH821-6628)

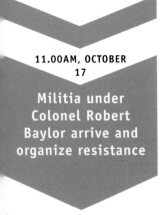

command of lawyer Lawson Botts and deputy sheriff/county jailor John Avis, both of whom had accompanied him from Charlestown. The men led by Botts were to "pass down the hill below Jefferson's Rock [named after Thomas Jefferson who, in 1783, found the view from the rock so impressive he wrote that it was "worth a voyage across the Atlantic"], and take possession of the Shenandoah Bridge." They were then to "leave a strong guard at that point, and to march down to the Galt House, in rear of the Arsenal building," in which it was supposed the raiders were lodged. Those under Avis were to take possession of the houses around the Armory buildings. As the latter group closed in on the Armory, a prominent farmer and slaveholder George W. Turner was shot dead by the zealous Dangerfield Newby, one of the sentinels at the Armory gates, while in the act of raising his rifle.

At this point, John Brown still had an opportunity to follow his plan. His escape route back across the Potomac and into the mountains of Maryland with weapons and a few freed slaves was still available, although he would have faced stiff opposition from the armed civilians and militia at the opposite end of the bridge. But instead of ordering a withdrawal, he seemed paralyzed by indecision and more interested in remaining at Harpers Ferry to convince his hostages, and anyone else who might listen, that he was not an outlaw and that his cause was just and righteous. Shortly after this, the Jefferson Guards could be heard approaching across the Potomac Railroad bridge. Armed only with the sword gifted to George Washington by Frederick the Great, Brown strode into the street in front of the Armory and ordered Aaron Stevens, Osborne Anderson, Dauphin Thompson, Dangerfield Newby, Shields Green, and several freed slaves, from the Arsenal with their Sharps rifles to join him. According to Anderson, Brown stated calmly: "The troops are on the bridge coming into town; we will give them a warm reception. Men! Be cool! Don't waste your powder and shot! Take aim, and make every shot count! The troops will look for us to retreat on their first appearance; be careful to shoot first." As the Jefferson Guards spilled out of the covered bridge and into the wide area in front of the Armory they saw the raiders drawn up in a line across the street ahead of them. "When they got within 60 or 70 yards," Anderson recalled, "Captain Brown said, 'Let go upon them!' Again and again was the fire repeated, creating consternation among the troops. From marching in solid … columns they became scattered. Some hastened to seize upon and bear up the wounded. They seemed not to realize at first that the raiders would fire upon them, but evidently expected they would be driven out by them without firing." The furious fire forced the Jefferson Guards back into the bridge leaving several of their dead lying in the street.

Observing the retreat, Brown ordered his men to return to their posts, although Shields Green mistakenly went to the Armory rather than the Arsenal where he had been for the past hour. While returning to the Arsenal buildings, Dangerfield Newby was shot in the head from the window of a brick-built store on the opposite side of the street by an armorer-turned-sniper named Bogert. Although the first shot knocked him to the ground

11.00AM, OCTOBER 17

Militia under Colonel Robert Baylor arrive and organize resistance

Newby somehow managed to return fire, only to be hit in the neck by a musket ball that cut his throat from ear to ear. "He fell at my side," recalled Osborne Anderson, "and his death was promptly avenged by Shields Green, the Zouave of the band." Green raised his rifle and brought down the sniper before he could withdraw from the window after delivering his second lethal shot. Angry citizens would later drag Newby's body into an alley and mutilate it horribly.

Alarm and panic continued to spread among the local population as the fighting increased in intensity. According to an account in a Pennsylvania newspaper, "During the firing the women and children ran shrieking in every direction, but when they learned that the soldiers were their protectors, they took courage and did good service in the way of preparing refreshments and attending the wounded." The informant, who watched from a

An escaped slave from South Carolina, Shields Green, also known as "Emperor," joined John Brown following a meeting in an old stone quarry near Chambersburg, Pennsylvania, on September 12, 1859. Although he had an opportunity to escape with Albert Hazlett and Osborne Anderson after the failure of the Harpers Ferry Raid, he chose to stay with John Brown in the fire engine house and was captured unscathed. He was hanged with fellow African American raider John Copeland on December 16, 1859. (Author's collection)

hillside as the action unfolded, continued that "all the terrible scenes of a battle passed in reality beneath [my] eyes. Soldiers could be seen pursuing singly and in couples, and the crack of the musket and rifle was generally followed by one or more of the insurgents biting the dust."

A momentary lull in firing occurred as the militia fell back into the Railroad Depot and on to the bridge. With his escape route now blocked, Brown determined to negotiate with his adversaries, and at about 12.30pm he sent William Thompson with hostage Rezin Cross who was to request a ceasefire and safe passage for the raiders back across the Potomac bridge into Maryland. As the two men approached, the armed citizens ignored the white flag of truce Thompson carried. Freeing Cross, they seized the raider and confined him in a second-floor room at the Wager House. Waiting a short while and wondering what had happened to Thompson and Cross, Brown sent his son Watson and Aaron Stevens accompanied by hostage Archibald Kitzmiller, the acting Armory superintendent, for the same purpose. But once again the citizens were in no mood for negotiation. Hollering for Kitzmiller to step aside, they peppered the raiders with bullets. Watson Brown was shot in the bowels and dragged himself back to the engine house where he eventually bled to death. Stevens was captured where he lay, having been shot in the chest and the side. He would have been treated the same way as Newby were it not for the intervention of Joseph Brua, one of Brown's captives, who ran out and pleaded that Stevens' life be spared. Thus, the badly wounded raider was carried into the Galt House, a saloon on the banks of the Shenandoah River, and given medical attention.

Meanwhile, at about 1pm Kagi and Copeland came under heavy fire at the Rifle Works, and attempted to send word to John Brown via William Leeman that their situation was becoming desperate and suggesting that they rejoin the main force at the Armory. Pursued by armed citizens and militia, Leeman abandoned his desperate mission and attempted to escape by crawling along a culvert and swimming out into the Potomac River. A dozen shots were fired after him and according to an eyewitness he clambered on to the rocks midstream and "partially fell, but rose again, threw his gun away and drew his pistol." When this misfired he drew a bowie knife and, throwing his heavy accoutrements off, lunged again into the water. As his pursuers continued to fire he threw up his hands and cried "Don't shoot," but militiaman George Schoppart fired his pistol into the young man's face regardless and he fell back on the rocks dead. His body remained on the rocks for the rest of the day and was riddled with bullets, serving as target practice for individuals and whole companies of militia.

Back at the Armory, Edwin Coppoc shot and killed Fountaine Beckham, mayor of Harpers Ferry, and agent of the Baltimore and Ohio Railroad, as he wandered unarmed too close to the main gates of the Armory. As an act of revenge, several militiamen dragged William Thompson out of the Wager House, shot him in the head and threw his body off the railroad bridge into the Potomac River. Elsewhere, Oliver Brown was mortally wounded as he retreated inside the Armory gates. According to James Redpath, he "spoke no word, but yielded calmly to his fate," and died a few seconds later.

The Perfect Steel Trap

By about 3pm on October 17, 1859, the reinforcements requested by Colonel Baylor began to arrive at Harpers Ferry, consisting of the Hamtramck Guards, commanded by Captain Vincent M. Butler; the Shepherdstown Troop, under Captain Jacob Reinhart, who were dismounted and armed with muskets; and about 30 railroad employees and "tonnage men" from Martinsburg led by Mexican War veteran Ephraim G. Alburtis. From his vantage point in the Arsenal, Osborne Anderson observed that "armed men could be seen coming from every direction; soldiers were marching and counter-marching; and on the mountains, a host of blood-thirsty ruffians swarmed, waiting for their opportunity to pounce." The two militia companies attacked across the bridge while Baylor ordered Alburtis to lead his men down Potomac Street into the Armory grounds from the rear. According to a report in the *Valley Spirit*, "Sharp fighting ensued, and at this time a general charge was made down the street from the bridge towards the Armory gate, by the Charlestown and Shepardstown [*sic*] troops and the Ferry people from behind the Armory wall. A fusilade was kept and returned by the insurrectionists from the Armory buildings." Whilst this was going on the Martinsburg men arrived at the upper end of the town and, entering the Armory grounds from the rear, joined the fray.

Of the events that followed, a Virginia newspaper reported, "Dashing on, firing and cheering, and gallantly led by Captain Alburtis, they carried the building in which the Armory men were imprisoned and released the whole of them. They were, however, but poorly armed, some with pistols and others with shot-guns, and when they came within range of the engine-house, where the *elite* of the insurgents were gathered, and were exposed to their rapid and dexterous use of the Sharps rifles, they were forced to fall back, suffering pretty severely." In his *Harper's Weekly* report, D. H. Strother added that "some twenty or more of daring spirits, headed by George Wollet, one of the railroad men, made a rash but gallant assault upon the strong-hold of the outlaws. Wollet broke open the door, and nearly succeeded in forcing himself in, but was shot through the left arm by a rifle-ball. The attack was repulsed, with a loss of seven wounded, three of them dangerously." Among the other casualties was Evan Dorsey, a 35-year-old conductor and free black from Baltimore, and engineer George Richardson, both of whom died later that day.

Osborne Anderson recalled: "As the strangers poured in, the enemy took positions round about, so as to prevent any escape, within shooting distance of the engine house and Arsenal. Capt. Brown, seeing their manoeuvres, said, 'We will hold on to our three positions if they are unwilling to come to terms, and die like men.' All this time, the fight was progressing; no powder and ball were wasted. We shot from under cover, and took deadly aim … and one and another of the enemy were constantly dropping to the earth." As the militia closed in, Brown attempted to maintain communication between the three points held by the raiders, and sent Jeremiah Anderson running to the Rifle Works through what must have been a hail of musket fire. After reaching his destination, Anderson was ordered by Kagi to return to the Armory with a message urging Brown to leave the town at once, fearing they would soon be "overpowered by numbers." Returning unscathed, Anderson delivered the desperate advice to those in the Armory and the Arsenal. In response, John Brown ordered Anderson back to the Rifle Works to tell Kagi to "hold out a few minutes longer," after which they

Based on a sketch by artist and reporter David Hunter Strother, this *Harper's Weekly* engraving depicts militia and armed citizens of all ages rushing to Harpers Ferry on October 17–18, 1859. (Author's collection)

HOW THINGS WENT WRONG

OCTOBER 16–18, 1859

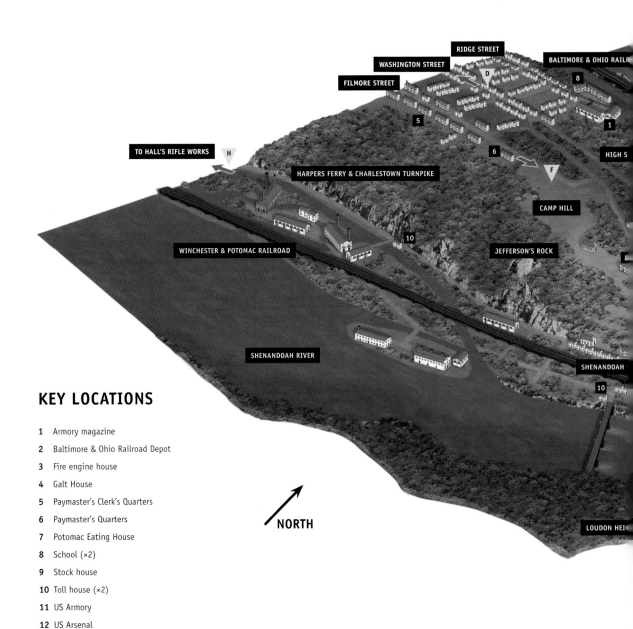

RIDGE STREET

WASHINGTON STREET

BALTIMORE & OHIO RAILR

FILMORE STREET

TO HALL'S RIFLE WORKS

HARPERS FERRY & CHARLESTOWN TURNPIKE

HIGH S

WINCHESTER & POTOMAC RAILROAD

CAMP HILL

JEFFERSON'S ROCK

SHENANDOAH RIVER

SHENANDOAH

LOUDON HEI

NORTH

KEY LOCATIONS

1   Armory magazine

2   Baltimore & Ohio Railroad Depot

3   Fire engine house

4   Galt House

5   Paymaster's Clerk's Quarters

6   Paymaster's Quarters

7   Potomac Eating House

8   School (×2)

9   Stock house

10   Toll house (×2)

11   US Armory

12   US Arsenal

13   Wager House Hotel

14   Water tank

EVENTS

A October 16, 10.35pm: Watchman Patrick Higgins is allowed to escape and raises the alarm.

B October 17, 1.30am: African American porter Hayward Shepherd is the first person shot dead during a raid meant to begin a revolution to free the slaves.

C 6.30am: John Brown permits the eastbound Baltimore & Ohio "Through Express" train to proceed on its way to Baltimore, following which the authorities in Washington, DC were alerted to the crisis.

D Dawn: Dr. John Starry rides over to Bolivar to raise the alarm and sends for help from the militia at Charlestown and Shepherdstown.

E 7.00am: Muskets recently moved to the stock house to avoid possible flood damage, and missed by the raiders, are smuggled out by Armory employees to arm the local citizens.

F 11.00am: militia commanded by Colonel Robert W. Baylor arrives on Camp Hill at Harpers Ferry and organizes resistance.

G 11.05am: With most of his men pinned down by sniper fire, John Brown fails to order a withdrawal back across the Baltimore & Ohio Railroad bridge despite having seized weapons and hostages.

H 11.30am–3pm: militia and armed citizens cross the railroad bridge and block off the escape route of the raiders. Other militia and armed groups surround the Hall's Rifle Works and occupy the Armory grounds, releasing prisoners. John Brown and the remaining raiders retreat into the fire engine house with ten hostages and are surrounded. Brown fails to negotiate a passage to freedom across the bridge.

I 11.00pm: Colonel Robert E. Lee and 90 US Marines arrive by train from Washington, DC.

J October 18, 7.00am: Brown refuses to surrender to Lt. J. E. B. Stuart. A Marine storming party smashes the doors of the engine house.

POTOMAC STREET

POTOMAC RIVER

SANDY HOOK ROAD

MARYLAND HEIGHTS

CHESAPEAKE & OHIO CANAL

POTOMAC RIVER

KEY

→ Routes of Brown's opponents

Raider Dangerfield Newby was shot dead by a civilian sniper shortly after the Virginia militia attacked across the Baltimore and Ohio Railroad bridge. Abandoned as the other raiders withdrew through the Armory gates, his body was dragged into an alleyway and horribly mutilated by the citizens of Harpers Ferry. (Kansas State Historical Society)

would "all evacuate the place," but before he got far along the street the runner was fatally wounded and crawled back to the engine house where he died shortly after. According to Osborne Anderson, "These few minutes proved disastrous, for then it was that the troops … came pouring in."

At the Hall's Rifle Works, one party of armed citizens led by 51-year-old watchman Henry Medler crossed the Shenandoah bridge and took up positions on the Loudon Heights side of the river. Another group was posted near the Winchester and Potomac Railroad track and at about 2pm they stormed the factory. Under heavy fire Kagi, Copeland, and Lewis Leary, plus Jim and another freed slave called Ben, scrambled out the back door of the main factory building and ran toward the railroad. Attempting to climb up on to the track, they were forced back by the fire of the militia posted there, and next made a dash for the river, splashing out towards a large flat rock. Exposed to a ferocious fire from both sides of the river, Kagi was killed instantly and his body floated away downstream. Leary was shot in the breast and stomach and mortally wounded. Both blacks were either shot dead or drowned. Copeland made it to the rock and tried to shoot James M. Holt, a butcher at Harpers Ferry, who followed after him, but his gun was wet and failed to fire. Holt tried to shoot Copeland at point-blank range but his pistol also misfired. The mob dragged Copeland ashore and prepared to lynch him, but Dr. Starry placed himself between them and the raider, and kept the crowd back until militiamen arrived and escorted Copeland to a safer place. Unable to flee any further, Leary surrendered just as Holt clubbed him with his pistol. Dragged ashore, he lingered about 12 hours from his painful wounds before dying.

With the recapture of the Rifle Works and the revelation that it had been held by only three raiders, plus two slaves, the citizens and militia realized that they had greatly overestimated the numbers they were battling against. Hence, no time was now lost in taking possession of the town and closing all avenues of escape. At about the same time, it dawned on John Brown that instead of having hundreds of allies, he was surrounded by thousands of infuriated enemies, and he made the decision to withdraw with the remaining raiders, consisting of Jeremiah Anderson, Edwin Coppoc, Dauphin Thompson, and Shields Green, plus Watson Brown – who lay mortally wounded – from the watch-house into the engine house. He also took ten of his 25 hostages in with him, leaving the remainder to eventually be released by the militia. Those taken were Colonel Lewis Washington; John Alstadt; Terence O'Byrne; John Daingerfield; Armistead Ball, master machinist; Benjamin Mills, master armorer; J. Burd, armorer; John Donahue, clerk of the Baltimore and Ohio Railroad at Harpers Ferry; Israel Russell, justice of the peace at Harpers Ferry, and George B. Schope, a 62-year-old cabinet maker of Frederick City, Maryland, who happened to be on a business visit the day the raid commenced. After getting them into the engine house, Brown announced ominously, "Gentlemen, perhaps you wonder why I have selected you from the others. It is because I believe you to be the most influential, and I have only to say now that you will have to share precisely the same fate that your friends extend to my men." Following this he ordered the remaining raiders to bar and barricade the doors and windows of the engine house, and knock rifle loopholes through the brick walls. He next sent Shields Green running through musket fire over to the Arsenal to communicate this development to Albert Hazlett and Osborne Anderson. Realizing that the situation was becoming desperate, Anderson attempted to persuade Green to stay with them. According to Hinton, Green "turned and looked toward the engine-house … and asked: 'You think there's no chance, Osborne?' 'Not one,' was the reply. 'And the old Captain can't get away?' 'No,' said both the men. 'Well,' [said Green] with a long look and slow utterance, 'I guess I'll go back to the old man.'"

Of events among the militia, Colonel Baylor recalled in a report in the *Alexandria Gazette* dated October 31, 1859: "The firing at this time was very heavy, and the insurgents could not have retained their position many minutes, when they presented at the door [of the engine house] a white flag. The firing thereupon ceased, and I ordered the troops to draw up in line in front of the Arsenal. During this engagement and the previous skirmishes, we had ten men wounded, two I fear mortally … we rescued about 30 of our citizens whom they held as prisoners in the guard-house – they still held in the engine-house, ten citizens and five slaves." Immediately after the troops had been withdrawn from the Armory grounds, John Brown sent a verbal communication to Baylor via Israel Russell, one of his hostages, stating that if the raiders could be permitted to cross the Potomac Railroad bridge with their hostages, they would free them and continue on their way. Baylor replied, "… if you will set at liberty our citizens, we will leave the government to deal with you concerning their property as it may think most advisable." A written response from Brown stated: "In consideration of all my men, whether living or dead, or wounded, being soon safely in, and delivered up to me at this point, with all their arms and ammunition, we will then take our prisoners and cross the Potomac bridge, a little beyond which we can negotiate about the Government property as may be best. Also, we require delivery of our horses and harness at the hotel." Baylor answered, "The terms you propose

William H. Leeman carried messages between the two groups of raiders until surrounded by militia, at which point he was shot attempting to escape across the Potomac to the Maryland shore. (Kansas State Historical Society)

This *Frank Leslie's* engraving shows William Thompson being thrown off the railroad bridge into the Potomac River by angry militiamen as an act of revenge for the shooting of Harpers Ferry Mayor Fountaine Beckham. Meanwhile, William H. Leeman is seen being used as target practice by the militia after his failed attempt to escape by swimming across to the Maryland side of the river. According to an eyewitness, a dozen shots were fired after him and he clambered on to the rocks midstream and "partially fell, but rose again, threw his gun away and drew his pistol." (Anne S. K. Brown Military Collection)

I cannot accept. Under no consideration will I consent to a removal of our citizens across the river. The only negotiations upon which I will consent to treat, are those which have been previously proposed to you." John Brown declined these terms. With the light fading fast, it began to rain heavily and Baylor decided to cease operations for the night and subsequently posted a perimeter of sentinels around the Armory.

The fortified engine house was described later that evening by a correspondent of the *Lynchburg Virginian* as consisting of "dead brick walls on three sides, and on the forth [*sic*] large doors, with window-sashes, above, some eight feet from the ground … The doors and walls of the building had been pierced for rifles, but it was evident that from these holes no range could be had, and that without opening the door they would be shooting in the dark." Outside, anarchy prevailed in Harpers Ferry as militia and sightseers flooded in by their hundreds, taking possession of the saloons and many of them shooting at random throughout the night. According to watchman Patrick Higgins: "The people, who came pouring into town, broke into liquor saloons, filled up, and then got into the arsenal buildings, arming themselves with United States guns and ammunition. They kept shouting, shooting at random, and howling." In his *Harper's Weekly* report of events, D. H. Strother concluded that "the armed and unorganized multitude largely predominated, giving the affair more the character of a great hunting scene than that of a battle. The savage game was holed beyond all possibility of escape."

Still guarding the pikes at the schoolhouse on the Maryland side, John Cook climbed an embankment to watch as events unfolded across the river. In his "Confession" during the subsequent trial he stated: "I saw that our party were completely surrounded, and as I saw a body of men on High Street firing down upon them – they were about half a mile distant from me – I thought I would draw their fire upon myself; I therefore raised my rifle and took the best aim I could and fired. It had the desired effect, for the very

12.30PM, OCTOBER 17

Brown attempts to negotiate a safe passage back across the Potomac

Led by Mexican War veteran Ephraim G. Alburtis, railroad employees from Martinsburg, Virginia, attack the raiders in the engine house at Harpers Ferry. Two of them died and four were wounded as a result of this action. Militiamen fire from the raised track of the Baltimore and Ohio Railroad, while frightened citizens can be seen running for cover beyond the Armory gates. (Anne S. K. Brown Military Collection)

instant the party returned it. Several shots were exchanged. The last one they fired at me cut a small [tree] limb I had hold of just below my hand, and gave me a fall of about fifteen feet, by which I was severely bruised, and my flesh somewhat lacerated."

Recovering from the fall caused by an amazingly accurate shot from across the Potomac, Cook scrambled back down the embankment and approached William McGreg, a lockkeeper on the Chesapeake and Ohio Canal. Cocking his rifle, he demanded to know what had transpired in Harpers Ferry, to be informed that the bridge had been blocked by militia, that all but seven of the raiders had been killed, and that two of them had been shot while trying to escape across the river. On his way back to the schoolhouse Cook stopped at the dwelling of an Irish family at the foot of the hill and was given "a cup of coffee and some eatables," and was mistakenly informed that "Captain Brown was dead." Finding the schoolhouse deserted on his return, he saw a party of men coming down the road from the direction of the Kennedy farmhouse. Ordering them to halt, he established in the half-light of dusk that it was Charles Tidd, Owen Brown, Barclay Coppoc, and Frank Merriam, plus a freed black. Informing them of the desperate situation across the river, the raiders decided it would be "sheer madness" to attempt a rescue of their beleaguered comrades. Returning to the Kennedy farmhouse, they slept in the woods close-by, where the remaining pikes were hidden. About 3am it was discovered that the freed black had slipped away. Fearful that he had gone to inform the militia of their whereabouts, the raiders scrambled over the mountain before dawn and crossed the valley to the range beyond hopeful they would not be pursued.

Across the river in Harpers Ferry, reinforcements continued to arrive after sunset on October 17. The Morgan Continental Guard, commanded by Captain Burwell Bassett Washington, arrived from Winchester, followed by three companies from Frederick, Maryland, under Colonel Edward

Also associated with Oberlin College and involved in the rescue of fugitive slave John Price, John Copeland, Jr, was captured while attempting to escape from the Hall's Rifle Works, and was hanged with Shields Green at Charlestown on December 16, 1859. (Kansas State Historical Society)

Shriver, commander of the 16th Regiment of Maryland Militia, consisting of Captain John T. Sinn's United Guards; Captain John Ritchie's Junior Defenders; and Captain Ulysses Hobbs's Independent Riflemen. Shriver had earlier traveled on the Baltimore and Ohio line as far as Gibson's Switch, near the east end of the Harpers Ferry Railroad bridge, to investigate the situation. Returning to Frederick to gather the militia, he proceeded back to Harpers Ferry "to show fight if necessary." Following their arrival outside the Armory, Shriver's men had "unanimously and warmly" favored a night assault, but Colonel Baylor objected as this would put the lives of the hostages in grave danger, so the Frederick troops settled in to their guard duties. Shortly before midnight, Captain Sinn was with some of his men on guard in front of the engine house when he was hailed by one of the raiders and asked to approach the building. Complying, he spoke with John Brown who once again asked if he, his men, and their hostages, might be escorted across the bridge, following which he promised to release the latter unharmed. Following this, he stated, he and his followers would take their chances in "an open fight." Sinn relayed this proposal to Colonel Shriver, who promptly approached the engine house and informed Brown that he was surrounded by an overwhelming force, and that his life was already "assuredly forfeited." The Maryland colonel urged Brown to release the "innocent unoffending gentlemen" he was holding as hostages, but Brown retorted that "he had secured them as hostages for his own safety and the safety of his men and he should use them accordingly." Shriver concluded that there were no further grounds for discussion and terminated the conference. Shortly afterward, Colonel Baylor sent Samuel Strider, a 66-year-old local farmer, under a flag of truce, in hopes that Brown might respect the approaches of a senior citizen, but he again refused to surrender as the rain poured down.

Having observed the unfolding events at the engine house while still concealed in the Arsenal buildings, Albert Hazlett and Osborne Anderson determined to make their escape under cover of darkness during the night of October 17/18. Amazingly, they managed to slip through the cordon of militia pickets surrounding the area and walked along the Winchester and Potomac Railroad. Following this they climbed the cliffs, crossed the heights, and reached a point on the banks of the Potomac River north of the town. According to Anderson, they "passed through the back part of the Ferry on the hill, down to the [Baltimore and Ohio] railroad, proceeding as far as the sawmill on the Virginia side," where they found a small boat and rowed across the Potomac. Reaching the Maryland shore, they passed under the Chesapeake and Ohio Canal via an archway and made their way back to the Kennedy farm in hopes of finding the raiders who had remained that side of the river. "But the old house had been ransacked and deserted," continued Anderson, "and the provisions taken away … Thinking that we should fare better at the schoolhouse, we bent our ways in that direction. The night was dark and rainy, and after tramping for an hour and a half we reached it about two in the morning. The schoolhouse was packed with things moved there by the party the previous day, but we searched in vain, after lighting a match, for food, our great necessity."

Somewhere along the way, the two raiders captured an armed citizen on his way home having been involved in the fighting against them at Harpers Ferry. Seizing his weapon, they forced him to travel with them until they reached the foot of Maryland Heights where, according to Anderson, he "begged us not to take his life, but let him go at liberty. He said we might keep his gun; he would not inform on us. Feeling

George Washington Kurtz was a member of the Morgan Continental Guards, of Winchester, Virginia, a volunteer militia company that arrived at Harpers Ferry during the evening of October 17, 1859. The Morgan Continentals later attended as an honor guard at the funeral of free black railroad porter Hayward Shepherd, and were also on duty during the execution of John Brown, standing within 60 feet of the gallows. (Courtesy of Larry Williford)

compassion for him, and trusting to his honor, we suffered him to go, when he went directly into town, and … informed on us, and we were pursued." Suspecting they might be betrayed, Anderson and Hazlett clambered about 100 yards up into the mountainside and hid in the rocks. A few minutes before nightfall on October 18, militia came in search of them. Anderson recalled: "They came to the foot of the mountains, marched and counter-marched, but never attempted to search the mountains; we supposed from their movements that they feared a host of armed enemies in concealment." Hidden amongst rocks and bushes, the raiders opened fire, wounding several militiamen. The exchange of shots continued for several minutes until darkness closed in and the troops withdrew back across the river to Harpers Ferry. The following morning Anderson and Hazlett headed north into Pennsylvania.

Taking Those Men Out

At Sandy Hook, Robert E. Lee ordered Lieutenant Greene to form his Marines and accompany him across the railroad bridge. Leaving the Baltimore militia on the Maryland side of the river for the night, he marched the Marine detachment across the bridge through the darkness into Harpers Ferry. As he led them behind the Wager House and into the Armory grounds through a back gate, he made a careful note of the layout of the government buildings. Once they had safely assembled inside the enclosure, the militiamen and armed citizenry were withdrawn and posted around the perimeter of the Armory grounds, while the Marines took over the task of securing the immediate area around the engine house as steady drizzling rain set in for the night. According to Colonel Baylor, commanding the Virginia militia, the volunteer forces were to "clear the streets of all citizens and spectators, to prevent their firing random shots" which might endanger the regular force.

Assessing the situation, Lee initially considered storming the engine house, but concern for the safety of the hostages during a confusing night action convinced him to wait until dawn. Taking little heed of tiredness, he planned his strategy for the next day. Realizing that the number of raiders had been grossly exaggerated, he decided there was no need to impose martial law and kept the President's proclamation in his pocket. Next he sent a telegraph to the Secretary of War apprising him of the situation and stating that he had halted the three companies of 3rd Artillery from Fortress Monroe at Fort McHenry in Baltimore to await further instructions. He continued his dispatch to Floyd by stating: "All the rioters now trying to escape. A man named Cook has escaped. They are barricaded in the Engine House within the enclosure of the armory. They have with them some of our best citizens, who they refuse to release… I have put the armory property in charge of the Marines and shall endeavor to secure and protect the rioters; they have killed several citizens and several of them have been killed." Lee also prepared his surrender demand to the leader of the raiders, to be delivered by Stuart at the colonel's order, and planned a course of action. Should the raiders refuse unconditional surrender, there was to be no bargaining with them. At a signal from Stuart, the assault party would batter down a door at the engine house and pounce on the raiders with bayonet and musket butt. There could be no shooting because of the danger to the hostages.

Photographed about 1860, this detail from a stereoview by George Stacy shows the partially repaired engine house at Harpers Ferry. One of the rifle loopholes made by the raiders has been bricked-up in the center-left column, and the wooden doors have been replaced by iron ones. The windows above the doors remain in a state of disrepair caused by the raid. (Library of Congress LC-DIG-stereo-1s01836)

Inside the fortified engine house, the remnants of the raiders awaited their fate. According to D. H. Strother, who interviewed several of the raiders after capture, during the night of October 17/18 Brown acknowledged that "all was lost; he knew that he had forfeited his life, and determined to sell it as dearly as possible. The courage of his men, too, began to give way, and they wished to surrender; but he urged them to continued desperation. One whom the idea seemed to strike for the first time, asked, 'Captain Brown, would this enterprise in which we are engaged be called "High Treason?" 'Very likely it would be so considered,' replied Brown. 'Then,' said the man, 'I will not fire another shot.' 'It will make no difference to you,' said Brown, 'except that you will die like a dog instead of falling like a man.'" The informant continued, "During the livelong night the voice of Brown was heard continually repeating, 'Are you awake, men? Are you ready?'"

Accompanied by Stuart, Lee assessed the situation at dawn on October 18. Selecting the force to make the assault posed a touchy problem in federal-state relationships as the raid was directed mainly at the slave states, even though Federal property was involved. Thus, Lee offered the honor of spearheading the attack to the militia. However, Colonel Shriver, commanding the Maryland troops, declined, stating: "These men of mine have wives and children at home. I will not expose them to such risks. You are paid for doing this kind of work." His only mission, he maintained, was "to protect the townspeople of Harpers Ferry." Colonel Baylor refused to offer the services of the Virginia Militia for the same reason, declaring that the Marines, whom he referred to as "mercenaries," should perform the task. (Baylor's actions were investigated by a court of enquiry in June 1860 but he was acquitted without charge. No action was taken against Shriver.) Lee next turned to Lieutenant Greene and enquired if his Marines would accept the honor of "taking those men out." Greene whipped off his cap and accepted the task with pride.

At about 6.30am Greene received his instructions. Twelve men, consisting of one sergeant, one corporal, and ten privates, were to form the storming party, with an equal number in reserve. In addition, a detail of two men, each of whom had been issued a heavy sledgehammer, was to accompany the assault party and batter down the center doors of the engine house. Twenty-seven Marines, with Greene and Russell at their head, gathered close to the engine house but out of the insurgents' line of fire to await Stuart's signal. In his after action report, Lee stated "the men were instructed how to distinguish our citizens from the insurgents; to attack with the bayonet, and not to injure the blacks detained in custody unless they resisted. Lieutenant Stewart [sic] was also directed not to receive from the insurgents any counter propositions. If they accepted the terms offered, they must immediately deliver up

A lieutenant colonel in the 2nd Cavalry, future Confederate commander of the Army of Northern Virginia Robert E. Lee conducted the final assault on the fortified engine house in Harpers Ferry which freed the hostages and resulted in the final capture of John Brown and his surviving raiders. (Author's collection)

This *Frank Leslie's* engraving depicts the moment the US Marines battered in the doors of the engine house using a ladder that lay nearby. First Lieutenant Israel Greene stands directing the action with drawn sword. The raiders fire through loopholes in the doors. The artist incorrectly shows two fallen Marines as none were killed or wounded at this stage in the assault. (Anne S. K. Brown Military Collection)

their arms and release their prisoners. If they did not, he must, on leaving the engine-house, give me the signal. My object was, with a view of saving our citizens, to have as short an interval as possible between the summons and attack." In preparation, Lee walked to a vantage point about 40 feet from the engine house, while Stuart stood in the center of the grass-covered enclosure.

Meanwhile, townspeople plus sightseers had flocked toward the Armory in order to watch the impending action. At about 7am Lee signaled Stuart forward, and about 2,000 pairs of eyes were fixed on him as he strode under a flag of truce towards the doors of the engine house to negotiate with Brown. He halted before the building and called for "Mr Smith," the name assumed by Brown when he moved into the vicinity of Harpers Ferry. The center door opened several inches and there stood Brown with cocked carbine aimed directly at him. Stuart recognized him at once from his tour of duty during the fighting between pro-slavery and Free-State forces in Kansas, and calmly presented him with Lee's unconditional demand for surrender, which stated:

> Colonel Lee, United States Army, commanding the troops sent by the President of the United States to suppress the insurrection at this place, demands the surrender of the persons in the armory buildings.
>
> If they will peaceably surrender and restore the pillaged property, they shall be kept in safety to await the orders of the President. Colonel Lee represents to them, in all

frankness, that it is impossible for them to escape; that the armory is surrounded on all sides by troops; and that if he is compelled to take them by force he cannot answer for their safety.

The surrender conditions were peremptorily refused by Brown, who once again proposed that he and his party should be escorted, this time by the Marines, to the Maryland side of the bridge, and pursuit by the militia should be restrained until he had begun his escape. While these exchanges took place, the cries of the hostages within the engine house could be heard, imploring the Federal officers to negotiate with Brown. But heard above all else was the voice of Lewis Washington, who called out in what Lee afterward termed "the old revolutionary blood of his fore fathers, 'Never mind us. Fire!'"

In the meantime the storming party led by Lieutenant Greene took up position on either side of the center door. As the lengthy parley ended and the doors were slammed shut, Stuart stepped backward several paces and waved his hat, giving the agreed signal to attack. Two Marines immediately sprang forward and swung at the doors with their sledgehammers, but the raiders had tied it with ropes and braced it with the hand-brakes of one of the two fire engines inside, and it resisted all their efforts. The Marines were therefore ordered to drop their hammers and, with a portion of the reserve, use a heavy 40-foot ladder that lay nearby as a battering ram. Rushing on with five men at each side, they dropped to their knees at the thunderous

This interior view of the engine house shows the hostages standing at left as the raiders attempt to fend off the attack. John Brown stands holding his Sharps carbine, while his son Watson leans against a fire engine mortally wounded nearby. A raider fires through a loophole in the wall while another loads his weapon. Shields Green holds a pike at the ready while more pikes are seen at far right. (Library of Congress LC-USZ62-132541)

blow in order to avoid the expected volley of fire when the doors gave way. As the ladder struck for a second time a ragged hole was smashed low down in the center door and the Marines rushed in. An eyewitness to events, D. H. Strother recalled: "The pent-up excitement of the multitude now burst forth in a shout that shook the air, and nearly drowned the sharp crash of fire-arms that received the stormers on their entrance."

The first man in, Lieutenant Greene recollected: "I instantly stepped from my position in front of the stone abutment, and entered the opening made by the ladder. At the time I did not stop to think of it, but upon reflection I should say that Brown had just emptied his carbine at the point broken by the ladder, and so I passed in safely. Getting to my feet, I ran to the right of the engine which stood behind the door, passed quickly to the rear of the house, and came up between the two engines. The first person I saw was Colonel Lewis Washington, who was standing near the hose-cart, at the front of the engine-house. On one knee, a few feet to the left, knelt a man with a carbine in his hand, just pulling the lever to reload." At that point Washington pointed at Brown and shouted, "This is Ossawatomie," referring to the nickname he had acquired in Kansas. "Quicker than thought I brought my saber down with all my strength upon his head," continued Greene. "He was moving as the blow fell, and I suppose I did not strike him where I intended, for he received a deep saber cut in the back of the neck. He fell senseless on his side, then rolled over on his back… I think he had just fired as I reached Colonel Washington, for the marine who followed me into the aperture made by the ladder received a bullet in the abdomen, from which he died in a few minutes. The shot might have been fired by some one else

Lieutenant "Jeb" Stuart can be seen standing to the right of the storming party waving his hat to signal the attack in this *Harper's Weekly* engraving. The ladder used to batter in the door is shown lying in the foreground, with the fatally wounded Private Luke Quinn nearby. (Author's collection)

in the insurgent party, but I think it was from Brown. Instinctively as Brown fell I gave him a saber thrust in the left breast. The sword I carried was a light uniform weapon, and, either not having a point or striking something hard in Brown's accouterments, did not penetrate. The blade bent double." Hostage John Daingerfield stated that Greene next struck Brown across the head "holding his sword in the middle and striking with the hilt and making only scalp wounds."

Meanwhile, about four more Marines had entered the engine house with fixed bayonets. According to Greene, they came "rushing in like tigers, as a storming assault is not a play-day sport. They bayoneted one man [Dauphin Thompson] skulking under the engine, and pinned another fellow [Jeremiah Anderson] up against the rear wall, both being instantly killed. I ordered the men to spill no more blood. The other insurgents [Edwin Coppoc and Shields Green] were at once taken under arrest, and the contest ended… My only thought was to capture, or, if necessary, kill, the insurgents, and take possession of the engine-house."

Three minutes of fierce action had ended a 32-hour reign of terror, and none of the hostages were harmed. The only Marine killed during the assault, Private Luke Quinn, received a fatal wound in the stomach as he followed Greene into the engine house. According to D. H. Strother, he turned away from the door, dropped his musket and staggered to the rear, where "he fell, preserving to the last his quiet, soldierly bearing." Quinn was afterward described as having "entered the service about four years since – being quite a young man. Fortunately he had no family." He was buried in the Catholic burial ground at Harpers Ferry with full military honors the day before the Marines returned to Washington, DC. Private Mathew Rupert received a flesh wound in the upper lip and had several teeth knocked out, but having his face well-bandaged appeared in the ranks for the return to the capital.

Brown's hostages were escorted safely from the engine house while D. H. Strother observed that "the bloody carcasses of the dead and dying outlaws were dragged into the lawn amidst the howls and execrations of the people. It was a hideous and ghastly spectacle. Some stark and stiff, with staring eyes and fallen jaws, were the dead of yesterday while others, struck with death wounds, writhed and wallowed in their blood." Edwin Coppoc and Shields Green were the only two raiders brought out unscathed.

AFTERMATH

The captured raiders, consisting of John Brown, Edwin Coppoc, and Shields Green, plus Aaron Stevens and John Copeland – who had been taken wounded the day before – were transported to Charlestown and imprisoned, under the care of the county jailor John Avis, who had assisted in their capture. After being declared fit by a doctor, John Brown faced trial for murder, conspiracy, and treason on October 27, 1859. Four days later the defense, eventually consisting of George Hoyt of Massachusetts, Samuel Chilton of Washington, DC, and Hiram Griswold of Ohio, concluded its case, having argued that Brown had killed no one, owed no duty of loyalty to Virginia, and thus could not be guilty of treason against the state. However, after hearing the case for the prosecution which was conducted over a period of three days by Virginians Andrew Hunter and Charles Harding, the jury took only 45 minutes to find him guilty of conspiracy, murder, and treason, and he was sentenced to be hanged in public on December 2.

During his last speech in court, John Brown stated: "I deny everything but what I have all along admitted, the design on my part to free the slaves. I intended certainly to have made a clean thing of that matter, as I did last winter, when I went into Missouri and there took slaves without the snapping of a gun on either side, moved them through the country, and finally left them in Canada. I designed to have done the same thing again, on a larger scale. That was all I intended. I never did intend murder, or treason, or the destruction of property, or to excite or incite slaves to rebellion, or to make insurrection."

During the month prior to his execution, he refused to cooperate with escape plans being devised by some of his New England friends and supporters. In particular, Silas Soule, a friend from Kansas, had managed to infiltrate the Jefferson County Jail authorities, offering to break him out during the night and flee northward. Brown reputedly told Soule that he was now too old to live a life on the run from the Federal authorities, and

John Brown lies wounded in the foreground as Shields Green and Edwin Coppoc, the only two raiders who remained unscathed upon capture, are dragged out to join him. The officer at left is probably meant to represent Lieutenant James E. B. Stuart, 1st Cavalry, who served as adjutant to Lee during the operation. (Anne S. K. Brown Military Collection)

he was ready to die as a martyr. His Virginia captors permitted him to write freely and receive visitors, and newspapers such as the *New York Tribune* provided detailed accounts of his remaining weeks. His letters to abolitionist groups served to strengthen the conviction of his supporters that his cause was just. Conducting himself with serene courage in the face of impending death, he impressed even those who disagreed with his cause. At 11am on December 2, 1859, Brown sat on his coffin in a wagon as he was escorted by the militia through a crowd of about 2,000 spectators to the scaffold which awaited him in a stubble field just outside Charlestown. As he mounted the wooden platform, he handed a note to a guard that contained his prophetic last words: "I, John Brown, am now quite certain that the crimes of this guilty land can never be purged away but with blood." Pronounced dead 50 minutes later, his body was later taken to North Elba, New York, for burial at the family farm. Present among the troops policing the execution was Thomas J. Jackson, commanding the cadets of the Virginia Military Institute who, during the next few years, would gain immortal fame as Confederate General "Stonewall" Jackson; and John Wilkes Booth, a private in the Virginia Grays, who would commit the final, tragic act of the Civil War by assassinating President Abraham Lincoln in 1865.

Four other raiders, namely John Copeland, Shields Green, Edwin Coppoc, and John Cook, who had been captured "much fatigued and almost starved" at Mont Alto, Pennsylvania, about 35 miles north of Harpers Ferry, on October 25, were scheduled to be executed on December 16, 1859. However, at 8.15pm on December 15, the alarm was raised which threw the whole of Charlestown into confusion when musket shots were heard in the vicinity of the jail wall and nearby guard-house. For two weeks, Cook and Coppoc had been cutting through their iron shackles using "an old Barlow knife" they had fashioned into a saw. They also made a crude chisel out of a bed screw, with which they succeeded, as the opportunity presented itself, in

Overleaf: "Taking those men out"
According to Lieutenant Israel Greene, the scene was thick with gun smoke when the Marines finally broke into the engine house. The first man through the door, Greene is attacking John Brown with his flimsy dress sword, while hostage Colonel Lewis Washington points Brown out to him. The other hostages are huddled to the rear with their hands in the air, following Washington's instructions, in order to be distinguished from the raiders. Dauphin Thompson is prostrate under the fire engine trying to take aim and about to be bayoneted to death by a Marine. Watson Brown lies dying in the corner near the hostages, while Edwin Coppoc and Shields Green also retreat from the onslaught.

This inaccurate *Frank Leslie's Illustrated Newspaper* engraving of the attempted escape of John Cook and Edwin Coppoc on December 15, 1859, shows them crawling through a hole they made in their cell wall and climbing down a drainpipe. In fact, the sill of their cell window was only about three feet above the pavement of the prison exercise yard. Once in the yard they had to scale a smooth brick wall, which they nearly achieved with the aid of the timbers of the scaffold on which John Brown had been hanged 13 days before, and upon which they were due to meet their end the next day. Their escape over the wall was foiled when a vigilant sentry spotted them in the gloom and opened fire, forcing them back into the jailhouse. (Author's collection)

removing the plaster and then the bricks of the cell wall behind their bed until they were ready to break through to the outside which was on the same level as the prison exercise yard. The bricks removed were hidden in the drum of a stove, while the dirt and plaster was placed between their bed clothing. Breaking out on the eve of their execution, they scaled the 15-foot-high smooth brick wall enclosing the exercise yard with the aid of timbers from the scaffold on which John Brown had been hanged, and on which they were due to tread the next day. Reaching the top of the wall, they were both spotted by a vigilant sentry who opened fire, forcing them both back down into the yard where they were recaptured by militia led by General William B. Taliaferro, who was to serve under "Stonewall" Jackson during the Civil War. As a result of the attempted breakout, the militia took possession of the interior of the jail and guarded the prisoners until they were executed.

Of the four convicted raiders hanged at Charlestown on December 16, 1859, African Americans John Copeland Jr and Shields Green met their end in the morning. Copeland was led to the gallows shouting, "I am dying for freedom. I could not die for a better cause. I would rather die than be a slave." Edwin Coppoc and John Cook were hanged in the afternoon. Although a group of African Americans in Philadelphia requested the bodies of Copeland and Green, their remains, like those of Jeremiah Anderson and Watson Brown, who died during the raid, were taken to the Winchester Medical College for dissection by students. Coppoc's body was sent to Ohio, while Cook's remains were shipped to his brother-in-law for burial in New York.

Having escaped from Harpers Ferry with Osborne Anderson, and assuming the name "William Harrison," Albert Hazlett was finally apprehended near Carlisle, Pennsylvania, having been overcome with exhaustion and blistered feet. Not convicted until February 11, 1860, he had continued to insist he was the victim of mistaken identity. A month after conviction, he was hanged at Charlestown, along with the wounded Aaron Stevens, whose trial had been suspended in November as Governor Wise considered handing him over to Federal authorities for trial in the district court in Staunton, Virginia. Their bodies were sent to New Jersey for burial.

Of the other four raiders who escaped on October 17, Osborne Anderson continued on to York after leaving Hazlett behind near Chambersburg, Pennsylvania. Riding a night train into Philadelphia, he received help from abolitionists, which enabled his return to Canada. Resuming the printing trade, he published *A Voice from Harper's Ferry* in 1861, which recounted his version of events surrounding the raid. Later during the Civil War he assisted in recruiting slaves for the US Colored Troops in Indiana and Arkansas.

Led by Owen Brown, Barclay Coppoc, Charles Tidd and Frank Merriam escaped to Canada. Despite poor health, Coppoc returned to Kansas in 1860 to continue the war against slave-catchers in the southern border counties of that state. Commissioned a lieutenant in the 3rd Kansas Infantry at the beginning of the Civil War, he was killed in a train wreck when Confederate bushwhackers sabotaged a trestle bridge over the Little Platte River east of St. Joseph, Missouri, on September 3, 1861.

Charles Tidd later lived in Massachusetts, Pennsylvania, and Ohio. Under the name Charles Plummer he enlisted in the 21st Massachusetts Infantry in 1861, and died of fever aboard the transport ship *Northerner* during the battle of Roanoke Island on February 8, 1862. Frank Merriam returned to Boston by the day of John Brown's execution. Persuaded by friends to go back to Canada, he afterward settled in Illinois. During the Civil War he recruited African American soldiers on the South Carolina Sea Islands and, with the rank of captain, helped organize the 3rd South Carolina Colored Infantry in 1863. Having survived the war, he died suddenly in New York City on November 28, 1865. Physically unfit for military duty, Owen Brown moved to California where he died of pneumonia on January 8, 1889 as the last survivor of the Harpers Ferry raid.

Support received from the "Secret Six," in the form of letters and documents, was discovered in a carpetbag at the

Entitled *The Arraignment*, and based on an eyewitness sketch made in the Court House in Charlestown, Virginia, by David Hunter Strother, on October 25, 1859, this engraving was published in *Harper's Weekly* several weeks later. John Copeland Jr and Shields Green stand at left. Although badly wounded, John Brown is shown in the foreground handcuffed to a jailor, while Aaron Stevens is supported by courtroom attendants, having sustained gunshot wounds in the chest and side. (Anne S. K. Brown Military Collection)

Charlestown was crowded with militia and sightseers during the trial of John Brown and his fellow raiders. This engraving shows the prison at extreme left, the Guard House at center, and the Court House at right where the trial was held. (Anne S. K. Brown Military Collection)

Kennedy farmhouse when searched by the Virginia militia. Of these men, Stearns, Howe, and Sanborn fled to Canada; Parker was dying of tuberculosis in Europe; and Smith suffered a breakdown and was confined for several weeks in the insane asylum at Utica, in New York State. Higginson alone stood his ground and made no apology for his role in helping to finance the raid. Eventually, an investigating committee chaired by Virginian James Mason found no conspiracy and none of the survivors of this group was punished for their involvement in the events leading to the Harpers Ferry raid.

7.00AM, OCTOBER 18

Engine house is stormed; raiders are killed or captured

CONCLUSION

To all intents and purposes, John Brown had failed miserably in his attempt to free the slaves in October 1859. He had committed a huge error by permitting the Baltimore and Ohio "Through Express" to continue on its way to Baltimore, thereby ensuring that the alarm was raised in the Federal capital. Furthermore, the quick thinking of Dr. John Starry in sending for help from neighboring communities meant that the raiders were contained at Harpers Ferry until the national government could respond. The killing of free black railroad porter Hayward Shepherd, despite strict instructions that civilians should not be harmed, appears to have influenced many slaves in their decision not to support and spread the revolt. The failure of the raiders to seize and secure the Armory stock house and powder store further enabled the local townsfolk to arm themselves and contain the situation until the militia and regulars arrived. Of overwhelming significance was the personal intent of John Brown to stay and fight rather than escape with freed slaves and captured weapons. As the militia closed in, the "avenging angel" concentrated on persuading his hostages and anyone else who would listen, that his abolitionist cause was noble and that he meant no harm, rather than carrying slave revolt into the mountains and beyond.

However, in the longer term the Harpers Ferry raid achieved considerable success as it made a deep impact on both the North and South. The event is considered by many historians to have been a major cause of the secession of the Southern States that led to the Civil War and the final abolition of slavery in 1865. In the North, it quickly became clear that John Brown had captured the imagination of many, who were deeply impressed by the courage with which he faced his trial, and by the eloquence of his letters and interviews from his jail cell. They were also deeply disturbed at his execution, and gathered together in cities and towns to pay tribute to the man and to condemn the South for hanging him. In Ohio, hundreds of people crowded into their churches for commemorative services. In Cleveland, the *Plain Dealer* reported that the bells remained silent out of respect on December 2,

John Brown ascends the scaffold followed by Sheriff Campbell and jailor John Avis. Future Confederate General Thomas J. "Stonewall" Jackson sits on his horse at rear left in command of the cadets of the Virginia Military Institute. Once a hood had been placed over his head, Brown was kept waiting nearly ten minutes while the Virginia militia marched and countermarched into position forming a square around the scaffold in case of a rescue attempt. Based on an eyewitness sketch by illustrator Albert Berghaus, this engraving was published in *Frank Leslie's Illustrated Newspaper* on December 17, 1859. (Library of Congress LC-USZ62-132551)

while a sermon entitled "the martyrdom of John Brown" was preached to a congregation of 1,400 people. On this occasion a photograph of Brown was exhibited on the center of the stage, to the left of which was the inscription "John Brown, the Hero of 1859," while on the right were the words "He being dead, yet speaketh." In Plymouth and New Bedford, Massachusetts, the bells were tolled at noon "in memory of John Brown." In Albany, New York, town officials ordered the firing of a 100-gun salute. Following a public prayer meeting held in the National Hall in Philadelphia, Pennsylvania, the *Inquirer* reported on December 3 that black abolitionist Robert Purvis declared, "Today a prophetic inspiration comes from the scaffold of Virginia, where now is sacrificed the Great Apostle of Liberty – the Jesus of the Nineteenth Century."

Mass prayer meetings were also held in Manchester, New Hampshire; and Worcester, Massachusetts, where the bells were tolled for two hours. African Americans held their own memorial services for John Brown in many cities. In Boston, all black businesses were closed; and in New York City they met at the Shiloh Presbyterian Church and declared that Brown died for the slave, "as Christ for the sinner." Blacks in Pittsburgh and Detroit also held ceremonies, eulogizing their dead friend. Funds were raised for John Brown's family in many communities, and for the families of some of the other raiders. And finally, in the weeks that followed the execution, Northern writers, poets, and intellectuals enshrined Brown in an almost endless procession of poetry, songs, essays, letters, and public addresses.

As early as December 16, 1859, a three-part drama by English-born actress and playwright Kate Edwards called *Ossawatomie Brown, or The Insurrection at Harper's Ferry*, had been performed at the Bowery Theatre in New York City. In a lecture entitled "Courage" given on November 8, 1859, Ralph Waldo Emerson had drawn the comparison between Christ and Brown, in which he suggested that the death of the latter would "make the gallows as glorious as the cross." On Independence Day, 1860, Henry David Thoreau wrote a speech entitled "The Last Days of John Brown" to be delivered in North Elba as the raider's remains were lowered into the grave at his family farm, in which he reflected that just before his execution "the man this country was about to hang appeared the greatest and best in it." During the Civil War, the song "John Brown's Body," originally called "John Brown's Song," provided inspiration for Union soldiers and influenced Julia Ward Howe's writing of "The Battle Hymn of the Republic."

The Harpers Ferry raid left a deep mark on the South also, and confirmed for many Southerners the existence of "a widespread Northern plot against slavery." Around the time of John Brown's execution, Governor Wise became particularly concerned as numerous cases of arson were reported in the area surrounding Harpers Ferry and Charlestown. Whilst Brown's body was being taken to the depot after his execution, great excitement was caused by

The bodies of those raiders killed at Harpers Ferry on October 17/18, 1859, were wrapped in the blanket-shawls they wore during the raid and buried beside the Shenandoah River in two large boxes. According to Oswald Garrison Villard, there they lay while "the hosts in Blue and Gray marched and fought over them" between 1861 and 1865. In 1899, all nine bodies, including that of Oliver Brown, were disinterred and moved to North Elba where they were laid to rest next to that of their commander. (Anne S. K. Brown Military Collection)

the arrival of a horseman with news that "Wheatland," the residence of George W. Turner, who had been shot during the raid, was on fire. The conflagration also spread to the farm and buildings of his brother William F. Turner, and some of his horses and sheep died mysteriously, having possibly been poisoned. Earlier, on October 27, the "Barn, Stabling, etc." of George Fulk, at Swan Pond in Berkeley County, containing $4,000 worth of wheat and hay, was lost in a fire supposedly started by a black arsonist. Five more cases of arson were reported from November 10 and 13. On the latter date, the stable and barn belonging to Charles Ruffin, son of firebrand secessionist Edmund Ruffin, who was to fire one of the first shots of the Civil War in Charleston Harbor on April 12, 1861, was put to the torch.

A considerable proportion of the Virginia Militia was mobilized prior to the execution of John Brown and his fellow raiders in response to these events, plus largely ill-founded but widespread rumors that various groups of abolitionists were preparing to rescue the "Harper's Ferry Conspirators." A total of 1,500 militia arrived in and around Charlestown during late November/early December 1859, to ensure that justice would peacefully take its course, and a similar number policed the hanging of the other raiders during the following months. As a result, the poor arms and equipment of the local Virginia troops became apparent. Indeed, Colonel Baylor, commanding the militia during the raid, reported to Governor Wise that the arms in possession of the volunteer companies in Jefferson County were "almost worthless," and that Colonel Moore had "not thirty pieces that could fire with any effect" among 135 men of the 31st Regiment on duty.

Similar inadequacies were found in other states as well as throughout Virginia. Aware that they might have to defend themselves against further Northern aggression in the near future, Virginia pressed for an increase in the annual quota of arms issued to their militia by the central government in Washington, DC. By the end of October, 1860, the State Adjutant General, William H. Richardson, had requested more than half of his state's quota for the following year, claiming that "the pressure of extra-ordinary circumstances" prompted his action, and President James Buchanan's pro-Southern Democrat administration complied. In December, Governor John W. Ellis, of North Carolina, requested 2,000 long-range rifles with bayonets which absorbed his state's quota for the next six years. All of the other Southern States also requested and received their quota of arms for 1861.

Farther afield, a wave of alarm and terror spread throughout the South that caused the militia in various states to reorganize and strengthen ranks in order to protect property and prepare for what Senator William Seward, of New York, aptly termed earlier in 1858 the "irrepressible conflict." While its militia system underwent considerable reorganization as a result of a "Military Convention" held in Richmond during January 1860, Virginia was not alone in producing a veritable multitude of new and active companies of volunteer militia, which were recruited in almost every town and village in the state. In Alabama a "Military Bill" was passed through the state legislature, which, according to the *Daily Confederation* of January 31,

DECEMBER 2, 1859

John Brown hanged in public

Entitled *The Last Moments of John Brown*, this painting produced by Thomas Hovenden in 1884 depicts John Brown descending the steps from the Charlestown jail on his way to the field of execution on December 2, 1859. Sheriff James Campbell and county jailor John Avis, who helped foil the Harpers Ferry raid, follow behind. The artist married Helen Corson, the daughter of an abolitionist whose father used his home as a stop on the Underground Railroad during the 1850s. (Fine Arts Museums of San Francisco, gift of Mr and Mrs John D. Rockefeller 3rd, 1979.7.60)

1860, "revived the militia." By November 1860, a "Military Convention" in Georgia had taken similar measures and had also recommended making provision for the establishment of a State Armory. In South Carolina, numerous Vigilance Committees and groups of Minute Men, inspired by their Revolutionary War forefathers, patrolled the countryside and plantations searching for abolitionists, who were considered "emissaries of John Brown."

To be a Southerner-in-arms commanded the respect and admiration of the entire community by the end of 1860 as the South prepared for inevitable Civil War. While the Harpers Ferry raid was viewed by many in the slave states as the act of a deranged fanatic willing to inaugurate bloody servile insurrection, Northern abolitionists saw the event as the work of a Christian martyr or "avenging angel" who was prepared to punish those who perpetuated slavery, and who sacrificed his life to secure freedom for all African Americans. Reflecting on the historical significance of John Brown and the raid on Harpers Ferry after the Civil War, Frederick Douglass stated: "John Brown began the war that ended American slavery and made this a free Republic. His zeal in the cause of freedom was infinitely superior to mine. Mine was as the taper light; his was as the burning sun. I could live for the slave; John Brown could die for him."

BIBLIOGRAPHY AND FURTHER READING

Anderson, Osborne P., *A Voice from Harper's Ferry*, Boston, Massachusetts (1861)

Barry, Joseph, *The Strange Story of Harper's Ferry*, Thompson Brothers: Martinsburg, West Virginia (1903)

Boteler, Alexander, "Recollections of the John Brown Raid by a Virginian who Witnessed the Fight," *Century Magazine*, Vol. 26 (July 1883)

Du Bois, W.E.B., *John Brown*, G.W. Jacobs & Co: Philadelphia, Pennsylvania (1909)

Earle, Jonathan, *John Brown's Raid on Harpers Ferry: A Brief History with Documents*, Boston, Massachusetts (2008)

Forbes, Hugh, *Extracts from the Manual for the Patriotic Volunteer*, W. H. Tinson: New York (1857)

Franklin, John Hope, *The Militant South 1800–1861*, Harvard University Press: Cambridge, Massachusetts (1956)

Hinton, Richard J., *John Brown and his Men with Some Accounts of the Roads they Travelled to Reach Harper's Ferry*, New York & London (1894)

Maryland State Senate, *Document Y, Correspondence Relating to the Insurrection at Harper's Ferry, 17th October, 1859*, Annapolis, Maryland (1860)

McClure, Alexander K., *Colonel Alexander K. McClure's Recollections of a Half Century*, The Salem Press: Salem, Massachusetts (1902)

McPherson, James M., *Battle Cry of Freedom: The American Civil War*, London, England (1988)

Oates, Stephen B., *To Purge This Land With Blood: A Biography of John Brown*, University of Massachusetts Press: Amherst, Massachusetts (1984)

John Brown's raid inspired Union troops throughout the Civil War and the 55th Massachusetts Infantry are depicted in this *Harper's Weekly* engraving singing "John Brown's Body" as they entered the Southern city of Charleston, South Carolina, on February 21, 1865. (Library of Congress LC-USZ62-105560)

Redpath, James, *The Public Life of Capt. John Brown*, Thayer & Eldridge: Boston, Massachusetts (1860)

Robinson, Sara T. L., *Kansas: Its Interior and Exterior Life*, Crosby, Nichols & Company: Boston, Massachusetts (1856)

Stauffer, John, *The Black Hearts of Men: Radical Abolitionists and the Transformation of Race*, Harvard University Press: Cambridge, Massachusetts (2002)

Sullivan, David, *The United States Marine Corps in the Civil War: The First Year*, White Mane: Shippensburg, Pennsylvania (1997)

De Witt, Robert M., *The Life, Trial and Execution of Captain John Brown*, New York (1859)

Villard, Oswald Garrison, *John Brown 1800–1859: A Biography Fifty Years After*, Constable & Co.: London, England (1910)

Zittle, John H., *A Correct History of the John Brown Invasion at Harper's Ferry, West Va., Oct. 17, 1859*, Mail Publishing Company: Hagerstown, Maryland (1905)

Plus various newspapers and journals including:
Alexandria Gazette (Alexandria, Virginia)
New York Herald (New York)
Frederick Douglass' Paper (Rochester, New York)
National Era (Washington, DC)

Shepherdstown Register (Shepherdstown, Virginia)
The Dispatch (Richmond, Virginia)
Richmond Enquirer (Richmond, Virginia)
Philadelphia Inquirer (Philadelphia, Pennsylvania)
Valley Spirit (Chambersburg, Pennsylvania)
The Sun (Baltimore, Maryland)
The Plain Dealer (Cleveland, Ohio)
Daily Confederation (Montgomery, Alabama)
Macon Telegraph (Macon, Georgia)
Jamestown Journal (Jamestown, New York)
Harper's Weekly (New York)
The Rights of All (New York)

INDEX